First You Grow the Pumpkin

First You Grow the Pumpkin

**100 cool things
to make & preserve**

a DIY in the Kitchen Collection

Ginna BB Gordon

Lucky Valley Press
Carmel California

Copyright © 2014 by Ginna BB Gordon
All rights reserved

Book & cover design by Ginna BB Gordon

Photos from the author's collection

Watercolors by Virginia Bell "Mama Ginna" Bragg,
from the author's collection.

ISBN 978-0-9856655-5-5

No part of this book may be reproduced in any form
by any electronic or mechanical means
including photocopying, recording,
or information storage and retrieval
without permission in writing from the author.

Published by Lucky Valley Press
PO Box 5474 Carmel California 93921 USA
WWW.LUCKYVALLEYPRESS.COM

Dedicated to
my brother, Jess,
and my niece, Kelly,
my foodie pals

CONTENTS

INTRODUCTION — 9
    How this started — 9
    Praline Pumpkin Pie — 12
    Pastry Cream — 12
    About me, Ginna — 15

WHAT'S IN THE PANTRY? — 18

EASY THINGS TO GROW — 23

PUMPKINS — 28
    Pumpkin Mash — 28
    The Best Pumpkin Pie — 29
    Pumpkin & Black Beans — 31
    Pumpkin Bisque — 32
    Pumpkin Lasagna — 33
    Pumpkin Muffins — 36
    Pumpkin Bread — 38

STOCK — 39
    Clear Vegetable Stock — 39
    Clear Chicken Stock — 40
    Dark Vegetable Stock — 41
    Dark Chicken Stock — 42
    Dark Beef Stock — 43
    Fish Stock (Fumé) — 45
    Soup Basics — 47

FRESH DAIRY — 49

- Evaporated Milk — 49
- Making Fresh Mozzarella — 49
- Paneer Cheese — 52
- Yogurt — 53
- Ghee — 57
- Butter — 59

FRUIT, JAMS & SPREADS — 61

- Apple Sauce — 61
- Apple Butter — 62
- Apricot Jam — 62
- Apricot Fruit Leather — 63
- Apricot Bread — 64
- Apricot Pie — 64
- Lemon Curd — 65
- Brandied Fruit — 66
- Cranberry Orange Preserves — 66

TOMATOES — 67

- Oven Dried Roma Tomatoes — 67
- Tomato Paste — 68
- Flossie's Spaghetti Sauce — 69
- Warm Tomato Chutney — 70
- Tomato Basil Bisque — 70
- Ketchup — 71

Tomato Salsa	72
Mango (or Papaya or Peach) Salsa	72

OILS, VINEGARS & DRESSINGS — 73

Infused Oils	73
Creamy Tofu Dressing	75
Miso Dressing	75
Lemon-lime Dressing	75
Minted Citrus Dressing	75
Dijon Mustard Dressing	76
Balsamic Dressing	76
Poppy seed Dressing	76
Yogurt Dill Dressing	77
Cilantro Dressing	77
French Vinaigrette	77
Green Goddess Dressing	78

CURING & PICKLING — 79

Citrus Cured Salmon	79
Meyer Lemon Preserves	82
Cornichons	83
Bread and Butter Pickles	84
Pickled Grapes	85
Zucchini Pickles	86

ABOUT FREEZING — 88

CONDIMENTS & SAUCES — 89
- Vanilla Extract — 89
- For Vanilla Sugar — 90
- Marie Gillan's Mustard — 91
- Aioli — 91
- Fresh Garlic Aioli — 92
- Hollandaise — 92
- Caramel Sauce — 93
- Enchilada Sauce — 96

HERBS, PESTOS & BLENDS — 97
- Basil or Cilantro Pesto — 97
- Ancho Chili Powder — 98
- Curry Blend — 98

CEREALS — 99
- Toasted Oat and Coconut Muesli — 99
- Great Granola — 100
- Granola Bars — 101

BREADS, PASTAS AND BAKING — 102
- Oatmeal Bread — 102
- Basic Pastry Dough — 104
- Pizza Dough — 105
- French Bread — 106
- Sourdough Starter — 107
- Sourdough Bread — 111

Popovers	112
Flatbread Crackers	113
Chocolate Chip Cookies	114
Legendary Cream Scones	116
Crumble Topping	117
Doggie Cookies	117
Kitty Treats	118
Pony Cookies	119
Chapatis & Tortillas	120
Homemade Flour Tortilla Chips	121
Buns for Burgers or Hot Dogs	121
Making Ravioli from Scratch	123
Mac & Cheese	125

MORE SWEETS & TREATS — 127

Christmas Plum Pudding	127
Rum Butter	128
Hard Sauce	129
Pastry Cream	129
Rice Krispies Chocolate Bars	130
Holiday Ornaments	130
Carrot Cake	131
Chocolate /Almond or	132
Peanut Butter Balls	132
Date* Nuggets	133
German Chocolate Cake	134

TEAS, DRINKS & TODDIES — 136
- Charles Dickens' Very Own
- Christmas Punch, 1847 — 136
- Chai Spices — 138
- Hot Toddy — 139
- A Good Posset — 139
- Teas — 141
- Sinus Anti-inflammatory Steam — 141

RESOURCES — 142
- An epilogue by Ginna: *21st Century Bookbinding* — 143

MEASUREMENTS & CONVERSIONS — 145
- Abbreviations
- Pinches to Spoons
- Gallons to Liters
- Ounces to Tons
- Fluid Ounces to Liters
- Grams to Pounds
- Mililiters to Gallons
- °F–°C Conversions
- Bar Drink Measurements
- Dish Measurements
- Cups to Spoons
- Cups to Gallons
- Inches to Kilometers
- Centimeters to Miles

Introduction

How this started

Once upon a time, not long ago, I asked my brother, Jess, for his recipe for Praline Pumpkin Pie. He gave me the list of ingredients, reprinted herewith, including my comments, in italics:

Jess's Praline Pumpkin Pie

1/3 cup butter
- *I s'pose I could make my own, but I'll skip that this time*

1/3 cup brown sugar - *Ohhhh K*

1/2 cup chopped pecans - *Fine*

1 lightly baked pie shell
- *I'll make my own - one in freezer?*

2 cans puréed pumpkin
- *OK, I have about 1½ cups of Sugar Pie Pumpkin Mash in freezer*

1/4 cup brown sugar - *OK*

1 can evaporated milk (1 2/3 cups)
- *I'll make my own*

1 egg yolk - *Fine*

1½ teaspoon pumpkin pie spices - *Fine*

3 oz package Jello egg custard mix - *What?*

…and so on.

He thinks I'm funny, my brother does. He says, "You are the only person I know who, when asked for a recipe, says, 'First, I'll grow the ... whatever." In this case, pumpkin!"

I met a woman a few years ago who, when told during our introduction that I make my own crackers, said, "Well, you must have a lot of time on your hands."

But, you see, it's my gig. Now that I am off the road from constant cooking and event gigs, and my son is grown, I work at home, growing herbs, writing about cooking adventures, creating oil infusions and body products, constructing baskets of willow from our riverbank, making bowls out of gourds, and dinner for two.

I am a very dedicated DIY girl. I like growing things that are otherwise hard to get, like canteen gourds, and red, deeply flavored tomatoes. Medicinal Herbs. Ancho Chili Peppers. Ooh, see, there's a big one. Ancho Chilies aren't available at our local Safeway. Sometimes I can find them dried in Hispanic markets. Anchos are Pasilla peppers allowed to ripen to a rich brick red. Once dried, they can be ground.... well, I am getting ahead of myself. More on Ancho chilies later.

Growing your own, making your own, distilling your own, preserving... there is great satisfaction in "putting up" a harvest from your backyard garden. Or a basket of apples, straight from the farm down the road. Hostess and Birthday and Holiday and Any Day gifts, from your garden and/or kitchen. Really. Your friends will love and remember you. It's a "straight from the heart" offering.

I know, I know, you live on the ninth floor and have a tiny balcony and a one-butt kitchen. I live in California, where the growing season is long, and the harvest bountiful. If I lived in Wyoming, I'd have a little hot house, for sure. But, even if you live in the city and have only a three square foot balcony and no green thumb and are a very busy and important person, careful shopping, a little kitchen consciousness and a bit of t.i.m.e. will serve you well.

Personally, I like my food prepared from whole, unadulterated ingredients. If I am going to ingest it, or put it on my lips, or spread it on my skin, or serve it to my friends and family, I want to know what is in it. I avoid anything I can't pronounce. No ranting about GMOs here, or preservatives in my orange juice, I just avoid those products that seem too mysterious, too far away from the farm. You are what you eat, so if you eat THIS, you'll be THAT.

I'll just say that the fresher and less adulterated the ingredients, the better for you. And your family. And all of your loved ones.

And besides, whole, fresh ingredients look, smell and taste better.

*F*irst You Grow the Pumpkin shares one woman's way of eating, feeding her family, being creative and preparing deliciousness from scratch. It is truly easier than you think.

This is my collection just for you, of the many, varied and simple things you can make, or grow, "put up" or concoct in your kitchen. It covers basics, like soup stock reduction and yogurt. And, Pumpkin Mash, of course. And even a good lotion for your hands.

It's not a diet, but a way of life. We need protein, we eat organic meat. We love fresh vegetables. We have stock in the freezer to enhance our rice or sauces.

We give hostess gifts and holiday presents made from our own herbs, by our own hands.

I offer this book as my contribution toward growing a better world. Just say, "I'll do it myself."

Oh, and here's Praline Pumpkin Pie, my way...

PRALINE PUMPKIN PIE

1/3 cup butter, melted
1/3 cup brown sugar
1/2 cup chopped pecans
1 lightly baked pie shell
1½ cups cooked mashed pumpkin

PASTRY CREAM

4 cups whole milk
8 egg yolks
1 cup granulated sugar
10 Tablespoons cornstarch
1/8 teaspoon salt
3 teaspoons pure vanilla extract

1 pastry shell, *page 104*

In a saucepan, warm the milk over low heat until it steams.

While the milk is warming, whisk together the egg yolks, sugar, cornstarch and salt until completely smooth.

Add half of the steamed milk, whisking constantly, to the egg mixture. Add the milk and eggs back into the rest of the hot milk, and heat for 1-2 minutes, stirring constantly, until the custard is very thick.

Remove from the heat. Stir in the vanilla extract. Chill before filling pastry. Makes about four cups.

Heat butter and sugar in saucepan until sugar melts and bubbles. Add pecans and mix. Spread into the bottom of a cooked pie shell. Bake at 425° for five minutes until bubble. Remove from oven and let cool.

Combine pumpkin, pastry cream and spices. Pour into pie shell. Chill before serving. Serve with whipped cream.

ABOUT ME, GINNA

You'll see the word chef before or after my name in reference to my books and cooking endeavors, but I've been hanging out in the kitchen with my mother since toddlerhood, cared for my own and others' children, started cooking for a retreat center in the early nineties, and have made cooking a part of my kit of nurturing ever since I could reach the stove. I am a cook.

I studied Ayurveda with Drs. Deepak Chopra, David Simon and Shamali Joshi. My education in the arts include the UCLA Design Program, the Guild of the Books Arts Carmel, Monterey Peninsula College and private sessions with myriad artists in and around California, including Alison Stillwell Cameron (Chinese Calligraphy), Tulku Jamyang Rinpoche (Tibetan Thangka Painting) and Louisa Jenkins (collage).

I am an artist, retired cook, author and gardener.

I have: owned businesses (the Book Studio, Ginna's Café, Ginna & Co.); managed kitchens and cafés in other folks' businesses (Rainbow Ranch, Calistoga; the Chopra Center for Well Being, La Jolla; the Thunderbird Bookshop, Carmel; Cornucopia Café & Market, Carmel); created events for non-profits (the Carmel Music Society, the

Carmel Bach Festival, the American Tall Ship Institute) and catered and cooked for many private clients, from stars to star gazers.

For two years, during one great cooking gig, I lived in a 400 square foot tipi made especially for me by Nomadic Tipi Makers in Bend Oregon. I have lived in many garden spots, but that tipi (with my 150 year old wood stove!) was the most beautiful, enjoyable and interesting abode I ever called home, even in rain, and wind and powerful elemental changes that kept me up nights coping.

Along the way, during a busy 30-year career in the food and event business, I have entertained myself and friends with art and garden parties, ceramic workshops, gifts from the garden and kitchen and herbal products for the body and table.

I've authored three other printed books about cooking:

A Simple Celebration: the Nutritional Program for the Chopra Center for Well Being (Random House/Harmony Books, 1997);

Honey Baby Darlin', the Farm (AmericaStar, 2011)

and ***The Gingerbread Farm*** (Lucky Valley Press, 2012).

My husband, David Gordon, and I *are* Lucky Valley Press, an indie publishing company that focuses on preparing books (our own and select others) for digital print on demand (POD) and publishing. We like books that have a heartfelt message, a vibrant meaning or a moment of beauty to share.

Each book in my memoir series (*Honey Baby Darlin' Book One - The Farm* and *The Gingerbread Farm*, so far) gives a glimpse of the many teachers and styles of cooking I learned as a retreat cook and café chef. Book three in the series, still un-named as of this writing, focuses on the professional years. Also in the works are *GB's Little Book of Ayurveda* (nuggets of information from my first publication, *A Simple Celebration*), and my first novel.

Visit our website to read more about us, Lucky Valley Press, and our authors and books.

It's just me and my own pots and pans in my kitchen, now (no staff of twelve), a big garden, a studio full of parts and tools and ingredients, and a sweet husband, David, who loves to test my kitchen creations. And who doesn't mind doing a few dishes.

WHAT'S IN THE PANTRY?

Every pantry tells a story.

It goes back to:

"You are what you eat,
so if you eat THIS
you'll be THAT!"

Here are the basic ingredients to cook
the way I do. I actually went through my
cupboards and just tallied up.
Assume everything is organic.

Dry Ingredients
Kosher salt
Sea salts
Flavored salts
Olive oil, both dark & light
Infused oils
Balsamic vinegar
Infused vinegars
Ghee (clarified butter)
Sweeteners
Dried herbs, spices
Non-fat dry milk
Baking Powder
Baking soda
Vanilla
Brandy
Sherry
Burgundy or other red wine
Peet's French or Italian Roast Coffee
Dried beans
Oats
Rice
Quinoa
Polenta
Gluten Free Crackers/Bread
Rice Noodles
Crackers
Bread
Sun-dried Tomatoes
Mixed Nuts
(my currents faves: roasted, unsalted cashews & macadamias)
Thompson Seedless Raisins
Pepitas (pumpkin seeds)
Sunflower seeds
Black Beans
White wine
Cumin seeds
Cloves
Allspice
Cinnamon
Stevia
Peppercorns
Thai Style Chili Paste
Coconut Milk
Pine Nuts
Dried Cherries
Dried Cranberries

Proteins:
Chicken (Roasted or uncooked)

Freezer
Beef & Poultry Bones
Fish or Shellfish Bones
Flours of choice
Pumpkin Mash
Stocks (containers & cubes)
Whey
Gluten free bread crumbs
Basil Pesto
Chicken sausages
Nut flours
Seafood selections
Lasagna Noodles

Refrigerator
Olives
Roasted garlic
Whole Milk
Cream
Cream Cheese
Yogurt
Eggs
Mozzarella
Parmesan
Butter
Buttermilk
Lemons or Lemon Juice
Salad Dressings
Preserved Lemons
Mustard
Mayo
Almond Butter
Fruit Preserves
Firm Tofu

Perishables
Basil
Cilantro
Tarragon
Parsley
Lemongrass
Tomatoes
Roma Tomatoes
Jalapeños
Celery
Carrots
Onions
Rutabaga
Turnips
Parsnips
Apples
Apricots
Prunes,
Plums
Pears
Peaches
Oranges
Garlic
Ginger

Containers & Paraphernalia
Olive oil bottles
Herb jars
Preserving jars
Paper tea bags
3 cup plastic freezer
  containers
Cheesecloth
Strainers
Large & Small,
  Deep Mixing Bowls
Parchment paper
Food Processor
KitchenAid Mixer
Tape
(for labeling containers)
Felt Tip Pen (ditto)
Tart Pans
9 x 13" baking dish
  (preferably glass)
Muffin cups
Large soup or stock pot
Large Sauce Pan or Dutch
Oven with lid
Candy Thermometer
Whisk
Incubator
  (Large Pot with lid
  will do)
Jar-grabber
Lid lifter
Wooden spoons
  & Ladles
Ball Jars
Water Bath Canner
Crockpot
White Bar Towels
Foil
Ziplocs, many sizes

Easy things To Grow

My husband, David, and I are blessed to live half a mile from the original Earthbound Farm stand in Carmel Valley. I trust their produce, and see much of it growing as I drive down the road toward town - tall stands of swaying corn, majestic sunflowers, bristly artichokes and golden marigolds. The squash and pumpkin display in September at Earthbound Farm is one of the fall wonders of Carmel Valley - the color, the variety, the bounty - when I see those piles of autumn abundance, the totem poles of squash, gourds and pumpkins, especially that first sighting every year, my heart does a little foxtrot in my chest. I catch my breath - the beauty just slightly overwhelms me. I'm serious. It's that beautiful.

On the Monterey Peninsula, there is a farmers market somewhere, every day of the week, so, I am happy to buy my kale or cucumbers or eggs from the locals. I say, let them battle with the gophers and ground squirrels. In addition to growing hard-to-find vegetables, I grow things that gophers and ground squirrels generally don't eat. (However, do remember that when the going gets tough for a gopher or ground squirrel (in July in California, for instance) - They. Will. Eat. Anything. I used to think that nothing, including gophers, ate gourds, which are foul, toxic and inedible, until I saw a green one, not quite ripe, slowly disappear into a gopher hole over period of 24 hours. Chomp. Chomp. Desperate gopher. The ground squirrels have been so desperate during our current drought that they have been nibbling the young, spiny artichoke leaves and completely dried out gourds.

Here are a few, easy to grow vegetables that are among my staples. Follow the instructions for your area. There is no big mystery to gardening. Food and water. Pest control. Proper environment. That's it. Pay attention, like feeding the cat every day.

And, use gopher baskets. And try a worm compost. It's easy and fun. Really. My worms (a couple of thousand, now) are named Vern.

Check out www.unclejimswormfarm.com.

Pumpkins

First, of course, is the Sugar Pie Pumpkin. I haven't grown a Jack-o'-Lantern pumpkin since my son, Michael, graduated from the eight grade, light years ago. Sugar Pies are for baking and cooking. They are small, with more pulp, less fibrous than the larger pumpkins, more tender, grow easily, but need some room (not nearly as much room as other pumpkins). I have tried them in barrel containers, and it does work, although more fertilizer is necessary.

Gourds

Gourds aren't good for eating (tell that to desperate gophers), but they're great for making artistic vessels and containers (the subject of another book...). They grow pretty much like pumpkins, but need a lot more room than Sugar Pies. Gourds plants love to climb, so trellises, fences, bamboo poles are handy. Heavy gourds, pumpkins and squash that climb will need support. I use nylons or sheer knee socks for little hammocks.

Squash

Like zucchini? Good, 'cause you'll be eating a lot of it if you grow zucchini. After one too many 24 inch, woody, fibrous, tasteless zucchini boats filled with rice pilaf, I learned to pick all of it when small. Zucchini Pickles! Yes!

Basil

Basil! Amazing stuff! Grow it five gallon containers and keep it in the sun. Give it plenty of water and regular fertilizer. Well-tended basil plants yield up to six harvests a season! And there are several good ways to preserve it (see Herbs, Pestos & Seasonings).

Tomatoes

Good seeds are essential. Mine come from www.tomatofest.com - check them out for Heirlooms!

Artichokes

Grows like a weed in Carmel Valley - two amazing harvest per year. Too many artichokes to count out of nine plants!

Herbs & Flowers

Most herbs will grow in pots easily. All they need is sun and water. So far I've found the even the squirrels aren't desperate enough yet to eat thyme, oregano, rosemary, etc. They will munch on basil and cilantro - anything with a tender stem. I keep mine in five gallon tubs inside the "Chicken Garden" - a transmogrified chicken run, completely surrounded in chicken wire, perfect for protection against marauding ground squirrels, rabbits and gophers, just in case.

Calendula is easy to grow and, as far as I can tell, gophers and squirrels don't care for it. Deer.... well.....

To learn about vertical growing on that three square foot balcony, check out www.growupvertical.com, produced by Gordon Smith, my Chopra Center colleague and author (with Reparata Mazzola) of *Save the Males*, the complete kitchen handbook, if you ask me, and since you are reading this book, I guess you did.

Pumpkins

Pumpkin Mash
The Best Pumpkin Pie
Pumpkin & Black Beans
Pumpkin Bisque
Pumpkin Lasagna
Pumpkin Muffins
Pumpkin Bread

Pumpkin Mash

Split open however many pumpkins you are preserving today.

Place pumpkin cut side down on a sheet pan lined with parchment. Bake at 350° for about 40 minutes, until cooked through and soft. Set aside. Too cool faster, turn pumpkins over to cut side up.

When cooled, remove seeds and discard, scoop out pulp and place in a bowl and mash with fork or in a food processor.

I bake off about ten sugar pie pumpkins, seed and mash it all and keep it in quart plastic containers or Ziplocs in the freezer. Be sure to name and date your frozen pumpkin mash.

THE BEST PUMPKIN PIE

1 cup heavy cream
1½ cups Pumpkin Mash
2/3 cup packed light brown sugar
2 large eggs
1 teaspoon ground cinnamon
1/2 teaspoon ground ginger
1/4 teaspoon salt
9" pie or tart pan; pie weights or dried beans
Parchment paper

Make pie shell (Pastry Dough, page 104):

Preheat oven to 350° with rack in middle. Roll out dough into a 15-inch round on a lightly floured surface with a lightly floured rolling pin; fit into pie pan. Trim excess dough, leaving a 1/2 inch overhang. Fold overhang under and press to edge of pan so pastry stands slightly above rim. Chill about 30 minutes, until firm.

Lightly prick bottom of shell all over with a fork, line with parchment and fill with pie weights. Bake tart shell until side is set and edge is pale golden, 25 to 30 minutes. Carefully remove weights and foil and bake shell until bottom and side are golden, about 15 minutes more.

Cool completely in pan on a rack, about 30 minutes.

Make the filling and bake pie:

Whisk together cream, pumpkin mash, brown sugar, eggs, cinnamon, ginger, and salt until smooth.

Put pie shell in pan on a baking sheet. Gently pour in Pumpkin filling. Bake until filling is set a few inches from edge, still wobbly in center, 50 -60 minutes. Cool in pan on a rack, 1 hour. (Filling will continue to set as it cools.) Pie is best the day it is baked.

Pumpkin & Black Beans

2 cups cooked black beans

1 Tablespoon olive oil
1 cinnamon stick
2 medium onions, diced
2 cloves garlic, minced
1/2 teaspoon cumin
1 teaspoon oregano
1 teaspoon sage
1 teaspoon marjoram
1 teaspoon mace
1/2 teaspoon pepper
4 oz. can diced green chilies
    or ¼ teaspoon Ancho chili powder
    or 1/2 teaspoon red pepper chili sauce
1/2 cup white wine
1 sugar pie pumpkin, peeled, seeded and cubed
5 chopped tomatoes
1/2 cup cilantro

Sauté cinnamon stick and onions in hot olive oil. Add garlic and sauté. Add pumpkin and spices, and sauté. Add cooked black beans and heat through. Just before serving, add chopped tomatoes and cilantro.

PUMPKIN BISQUE

3 sugar pie pumpkins, washed, cut in quarters or
2 quarts Pumpkin Mash, page 28
3 tablespoons ghee
1 teaspoon brown mustard seeds
1 teaspoon cumin seeds
3 carrots, chopped
3 stalks celery, chopped
1 yellow onion, chopped
1 clove garlic, minced
2 inch piece ginger root, peeled and minced or crushed
1 Tablespoon Thai-style chili paste
1 teaspoon cinnamon
1/2 teaspoon cloves
1 teaspoon kosher salt
4-5 cups veggie stock
1 cup coconut milk
1 pint plain yogurt

Place pumpkin on a sheet pan lined with parchment. Bake at 350° for about 40 minutes, until cooked through and soft. Set aside. When cooled, remove seeds and discard, scoop out pulp and place in a bowl.

Heat the ghee in a large pot. Add mustard and cumin seeds and stir until they begin to pop. Add the carrots, celery, onion, garlic, ginger root, chili paste, cinnamon and cloves and stir.

Add the squash pulp and blend well. Slowly add 2 or 3 cups stock. Blend well. Using a handheld soup blender or food processor, process until smooth. Add more stock to make desired consistency. Add coconut milk to taste. Salt to taste. Serve with dollops of yogurt (thin the yogurt with water or milk if it is heavier than your soup).

PUMPKIN LASAGNA

1 pound fresh lasagna noodles
4 Tablespoons olive oil
1 onion, coarsely chopped
3 carrots, chopped
3 stalks celery, chopped
1 pound baby spinach
2 garlic cloves, minced
Kosher salt and freshly ground pepper
4 cups Pumpkin Mash, page 28
1/2 cup toasted pine nuts
1 cup chicken or veggie stock (pages 39-45)
1/4 cup heavy cream
1/2 cup roasted garlic
4 cups fresh Mozzarella (page 49), drained
1 cup pesto, fresh or frozen
1 cup grated Parmesan cheese

Preheat the oven to 400°

If using fresh noodles (which I hope you are!), skip this next bit: In a large pot of boiling salted water, cook the lasagna noodles until just soft, about 3 minutes. Drain well and transfer the noodles to a baking sheet. Toss the noodles with olive oil to prevent them from sticking together.

In a large skillet, heat the 2 tablespoons of olive oil. Add the onion, carrots and celery (the Mirapoix, page 47) and cook over moderately low heat until softened, about 7 minutes. Add the pumpkin mash and stock. Simmer five minutes. Place in food processor with pine nuts and puree until fairly smooth, adding cream at the end to smooth it out. Set aside.

In the same skillet, add the baby spinach with remaining 2 Tablespoons of olive oil and wilt quickly.

In a sprayed or oiled 9-x-13-inch baking dish, spoon 1/4 of the pumpkin sauce in an even layer. Arrange 3 or 4 lasagna noodles in the dish, overlapping them slightly. Spread another 1/4 of the pumpkin mixture over the noodles in an even layer. Top with the wilted spinach, roasted garlic and a nice even layer of Mozzarella. Add another layer of noodles. Add another 1/4 of the pumpkin sauce and spread the pesto over it as evenly as possible. Add the third layer of noodles and cover completely with the rest of the pumpkin sauce.

Sprinkle liberally with Parmesan cheese.

Cover the lasagna with foil and bake for 40 –50 minutes, until bubbling and browned on top. Lasagna can be assembled a day ahead and refrigerated. Remove from fridge about one hour before baking.

Pumpkin Muffins

1 cup flour
1/2 cup sugar
2 teaspoons baking powder
1½ teaspoon cinnamon
1/4 teaspoon ground ginger
1/2 teaspoon nutmeg
1/2 teaspoon salt
4 Tablespoons butter, cut into pieces
1 cup Pumpkin Mash
1/2 cup evaporated milk
1 egg
1½ teaspoon vanilla
1/2 cup golden raisins

Spice Top

2 Tablespoons sugar
1 teaspoon cinnamon
1/4 teaspoon nutmeg

Frosting

1/4 cup butter, softened
4 oz. cream cheese
1/2 pound powdered sugar
1/2 teaspoon vanilla

Preheat oven to 400°

Prepare 12 muffins cups (spray, butter, whatever)

Sift flour, sugar, baking powder, cinnamon, ginger, nutmeg, and salt. Place in food processor, add butter and blend until incorporated into dry ingredients.

In a separate bowl, mix together Pumpkin Mash (page 28), evaporated milk, egg and vanilla. Pour pumpkin mixture gently into the flour mixture. Add raisins. Fold gently until mixture is just combined.

Pour into prepared muffin cups about 1/2 full. Sprinkle with remaining cinnamon-sugar-nutmeg mixture.

Bake for 25 minutes. Cool in pan for 15 minutes. Remove from pan.

Mix all frosting ingredients in food processor or in KitchenAid until soft and smooth. Spread or pipe onto muffins.

PUMPKIN BREAD

3 cups all-purpose flour
1½ teaspoon baking soda
1/4 teaspoon salt
2 teaspoons cinnamon
1/2 teaspoon nutmeg
1/4 teaspoon ginger
1/4 teaspoon all-spice
1/4 cup butter, softened
2¼ cup sugar
3 eggs
2 cups Pumpkin Mash (page 28)
2 teaspoons vanilla extract
1 cup buttermilk

Preheat oven to 275°

Sift together flour, baking soda, salt, cinnamon, nutmeg, ginger, and allspice. Set aside.

In a large bowl, cream together butter and sugar. Mix in eggs. Mix in the Pumpkin Mash. Add vanilla. Stir in half of the dry mixture into the wet mixture just until combine.

Add half of the buttermilk.

Add in the rest of the dry mixture and then stir in the rest of the buttermilk. Pour batter into two greased and floured loaf pans.

Bake for 1+ hours, or until golden and a toothpick inserted into the center comes out clean. Be careful not to over bake and keep in mind that the bread will continue to bake as it cools down.

Stock

Opening my freezer to see quart containers and iced cubes of stock feels as good as a closet full of clothes, gas in the car, a stacked cord of firewood.

Clear Vegetable Stock

Makes 4 quarts

2 carrots, cut in large chunks
3 celery stalks, cut in large chunks
2 large white onions, quartered, skins on
1 head of garlic, halved
1 each rutabaga, parsnip, turnip, halved
2 bay leaves
1 teaspoon salt
4 quarts water

Brush and clean the vegetables and place in a large stockpot over medium heat. Add about 4 quarts water. Toss in the bay leaves and salt and allow it to slowly come to a simmer. Lower the heat to medium-low and gently simmer for 3 hours, partially covered.

Carefully strain the stock through a fine sieve into another pot to remove the vegetable solids. Use the stock immediately or if you plan to store it, place the pot in a sink full of ice water and stir to cool down the stock. Cover and refrigerate for up to one week or freeze in containers.

CLEAR CHICKEN STOCK
Makes four quarts

1 chicken, plucked and washed
2 carrots, cut in large chunks
3 celery stalks, cut in large chunks
2 large white onions, quartered
1 head of garlic, halved
1 each: rutabaga, parsnip, turnip, halved
2 bay leaves
1 teaspoon salt
3 quarts water

Brush and clean the vegetables and place in a large stockpot over medium heat. Add about 4 quarts water. Gently place whole chicken in the pot. Toss in the bay leaves and salt and allow it to slowly come to a simmer.

Lower the heat to medium low and gently simmer for 1 hour, partially covered.

Carefully strain the stock through a fine sieve into another pot to remove the vegetable solids. Use the stock immediately or to store it, place the pot in a sink full of ice water and stir to cool down the stock. Use the chicken meat in a finished soup.

Cover and refrigerate for up to one week or freeze.

Dark Vegetable Stock
Makes four quarts

Use this stock when a deep color and strong, smoky flavors will enhance the recipe, like a vegetarian version of French Onion Soup. It can be kept for up to 5 days in the refrigerator, or frozen for up to 2 months.

2 yellow onions, unpeeled, quartered
6 shallots
8 cloves garlic, unpeeled
1 carrot, washed,
brushed and cut in half
six stalks celery, cut in half
2 each parsnips, turnips, rutabagas,
washed, brushed and cut in half
5-6 quarts water
salt and pepper
lemongrass stalk

Preheat an oven to 400°

Spread the vegetables on a baking sheet. Toss lightly with olive oil, salt and pepper. Place in the oven and roast, turning the vegetables at least once during cooking, until the vegetables are well darkened on some surfaces, about 55 minutes, using parchment preserves the pan.

Transfer the vegetables to a large stock pot and fill with water. Bring barely to a boil, then reduce the heat to low and simmer uncovered without allowing the water to bubble, for about 3 hours. Don't ever boil any stock—the protein particles will start to separate and fall apart, making the stock cloudy. The stock should be deeply colored and very aromatic. Add more water if necessary. Strain through a fine-mesh sieve into containers. Let cool. Cap tightly, and refrigerate or freeze.

DARK CHICKEN STOCK

1 chicken, cut in pieces
2 carrots, cut in large chunks
3 celery stalks, cut in large chunks
2 large white onions, quartered
1 head of garlic, halved
1 each rutabaga, parsnip, turnip, halved
Dried herbs
2 bay leaves
1 teaspoon salt
3 quarts water

Cover two baking trays with parchment. Place chicken pieces on one, the vegetables on the other. Coat with olive oil, salt and herbs. Roast in 350° oven for about an hour. Remove from oven and cool to a handling point. Place roasted chicken pieces and vegetables in a large stockpot over medium heat. Add about 4 quarts water. Toss in the bay leaves and salt and allow it to slowly come to a simmer. Lower the heat to medium low and gently simmer for 3 hours, partially covered. Be careful not to boil the stock. This causes the protein bits to separate and cloud an otherwise beautiful stock. Remove from heat and cool slightly before the next step.

Carefully strain the stock through a fine sieve into another pot to remove the solids. Use the stock immediately or to store it, place the pot in a sink full of ice water and stir to cool down the stock. Cover and refrigerate for up to one week or freeze.

DARK BEEF STOCK

2 pounds beef bones
2 carrots, cut in large chunks
3 celery stalks, cut in large chunks
2 large white onions, quartered
1 head of garlic, halved
1 each rutabaga, parsnip, turnip, halved
2 bay leaves
1 teaspoon salt
3 quarts water

Cover two baking trays with parchment. Place bones on one, the vegetables on the other. Coat with olive oil, salt and herbs. Roast in 350° oven for about an hour. Remove from oven and Cool to a handling point. Place roasted bones and vegetables in a large stockpot over medium heat. Add about 4 quarts water.

Toss in the bay leaves and salt and allow it to slowly come to a simmer. Lower the heat to medium-low and gently simmer for 3 hours, partially covered. Be careful not to boil the stock. This causes the protein bits to separate and cloud an otherwise beautiful stock. Remove from heat and cool slightly before the next step.

Carefully strain the stock through a fine sieve into another pot to remove the solids. Use the stock immediately or to store it, place the pot in a sink full of ice water and stir to cool down the stock. Cover and refrigerate for up to one week or freeze.

Fish Stock (Fumé)

Makes 1 gallon

Fish stock, or fumé, is quick and easy to make, and is a really magnificent base for fish soups, chowders, seafood risotto, any number of sauces, and many other uses.

The best fish bones to use are those from mild, lean, white fish like halibut, cod or flounder. Fish to avoid are salmon, trout, mackerel or other oily, fatty fish.

4 lbs fish bones (or substitute 4 pounds shellfish shells)
1 gallon water
1 cup white wine
1 stalk celery, chopped
1 carrot, peeled and chopped
1 yellow onion, peeled and chopped
2 Tablespoons butter
1 spice sachet containing:
2-3 whole peppercorns
3-4 parsley stems
1 bay leaf
1 whole clove
1 pinch dried thyme

Make the sachet by tying the thyme, peppercorns, clove, parsley stems and bay leaf into a piece of cheesecloth.

In a heavy-bottomed stock pot or soup pot, heat the butter over medium heat.

Lower the heat, add the vegetables and sweat, with the lid on, for about 5 minutes or until the onions are softened and slightly translucent. Don't brown the vegetables, though.

Add the fish bones and sweat for another couple of minutes, covered, until the bones are slightly opaque.

Add the wine and bring up the heat until it starts to simmer. Then add the sachet and let simmer for 30-45 minutes.

Strain (remove fish bones first if that makes it easier), cool and refrigerate.

Soup Basics

Every day is different. Especially in the garden. Use this basic recipe for good vegetable soup from the fresh ingredients in the basket (and what you find in the fridge and the pantry) every day.

The Pot:
Heavy bottomed, Large, non-reactive, stainless steel (not aluminum).

Fat:
Use ghee, butter, olive oil or sunflower oil. If no fat required, use small amount of stock.

Seeds and spices:
For Indian or Asian soups, pop seeds and bloom spices (mustard, fenugreek, cinnamon, cardamom, coriander, cumin, etc.) in hot fat before next step. Spices may be coarsely ground with mortar and pestle if desired.

Mirapoix (onion 50%, carrots 25%, celery 25%):

This mixture was named for CPGF (Charles Pierre Gaston François) de Lévis, Duke of Mirapoix, whose ancestors had been lords of Mirepoix in Languedoc since the 11th century.

CPFG was an 18th century maréchal, or marshal, of France and an ambassador for the French king, Louis XV.

Lord Mirapoix's chef de cuisine established carrots, onions, celery and perhaps garlic as the base to his every sauce and soup, and called it Mirapoix, in honor of his patron.

Always begin soup, and some sauces, with the base of Mirapoix to add depth and intense flavor.

When "sweating" the Mirapoix, be careful not to let it brown - that would make it *caramelized*. Size of veggies effects cooking time. Large chunks may be used for a soup that is to be blended.

Herbs:

Add fresh or dried herbs now. Use the woody, hard herbs here, such as rosemary, bay, thyme or sage.

Liquid:

Add a bit more liquid than you think you need – it will reduce in volume as it cooks. Use rich vegetable stock, white wine, liquid from other cooked veggies or potatoes.

Beans, rice or starchy vegetables:

For a thick or more substantial soup, add cooked and cooled beans, potatoes, rice or lentils.

Fresh Dairy

Evaporated Milk

Simmer 2 ¼ cups of regular milk until it reduces to 1 cup.

Evaporated milk can also be replaced by combining three parts whole milk and 1 part half-and-half.

Making Fresh Mozzarella

A gallon of whole raw or un-homogenized milk.
Pasteurized milk is OK, but it is not smooth and creamy - it will resemble Ricotta.

1½ teaspoons of citric acid powder- loose powder or tablets.

1/4 teaspoon liquid vegetable rennet combined with 1 cup of water, or 1/4 vegetable rennet tablet, crushed and dissolved in a cup of water.

1 to 2 teaspoons of kosher salt, to taste.

Sprinkle the citric acid powder (or crushed tablets) into a cool, empty, large non-reactive stockpot. Pour 1/4 cup water over it and stir it to dissolve.

Pour the milk into the citric acid solution and stir. Put the pot over medium-low heat and bring to 90° (using a candy thermometer). The milk begins to curdle.

When the milk reaches 90°, remove the pot from the burner and pour in the rennet mixed with water. Stir the mixture gently for 30 seconds.

Place the lid on the pot and let stand for five minutes. The mixture should resemble a very soft custard, which firms up, but is still very loose.

With a long spatula, cut the curd into a 1-inch checkerboard pattern, making lines across, then lines in the other direction.

Return the pot to the burner over medium heat and stir gently until the temperature of the whey (the greenish liquid that separates from the curd) reaches 105°. Use a slotted spoon to transfer the curd to a colander lined with cheesecloth and set over a bowl. Allow the whey to drain from the curd overnight.

Remove the cheese and gently squeeze it a few times to drain off more excess whey, which you can save for other things.

Knead and stretch the curd a bit to drain more whey.
Knead in the salt and roll it under itself until it forms a neat ball. Then set the ball into an ice water bath and let it rest in there until totally cool. Set it on a plate and sprinkle with herbs, salt, pepper, and crushed red pepper over the top.

Keeps in brine (salt water) for a week.

PANEER CHEESE
Similar to Cottage Cheese and Ricotta

1 gallon organic milk
1 quart cultured buttermilk
A squeeze of lemon juice

In a large, heavy bottomed pot, bring the milk to a boil over medium heat. Do not let it boil over. At the first signs of a boil, it will begin to foam. Remove the pot from the heat and add the buttermilk. Stir gently. Squeeze in the lemon juice. The curds and whey will begin to separate.

Set aside (about 30 minutes) while you line a large colander with several layers of cheesecloth, big enough to twist around the cheese, about 12 x 12 inches.

Gently pour the curds into the cheesecloth-lined colander and strain. When completely cooled, gather the corners of the cheesecloth and twist around the cheese, gently squeezing, expelling liquid. The more liquid expelled, the harder the cheese. For ricotta style, squeeze less and put in an airtight container and refrigerate. For paneer, squeeze until you can't squeeze anymore, knead the cheese for 20 seconds and press into a shallow pan to form a square or rectangle – cut into pieces for frying, etc.

Makes 2 cups.

YOGURT

1½ gallons whole milk (*Use 1%, or whatever you want. I like whole milk.*)

1 cup organic commercial active culture yogurt. (*After making yogurt, always set aside one cup for the next batch.*)

spatula

thermometer (*A candy thermometer that clips on the side of the pan is best*)

small bowl and a whisk

a large dutch oven to heat and incubate the milk

Heat

In your dutch oven, heat the milk to just below boiling, 200°F. Stir gently as it heats to make sure the bottom doesn't scorch and the milk doesn't boil over.

This heating step changes the protein structure in the milk so it sets as a solid instead of separating like paneer cheese.

Let the milk cool to 112°F - 115°F. This takes about 45 minutes after the pot is removed from the heat. Use the candy thermometer.

Inoculate

Pour about a cup of the warm milk into a small bowl and whisk it with the yogurt culture. Once it's smooth, whisk this back into the pan of milk.

Incubate

Warm the oven to about 115°. Put the lid on the dutch oven with your inoculated milk and wrap the pot in a few layers of towels, to insulate the pot and keep it warm. Set in the warmed (but turned off!) oven and set the timer. Don't peek. The milk should stay at about 110°F until it has set, 4-7 hours.

The texture should be creamy, like custard, and the flavor tart. Overnight yogurt is rich and tangy.

Cool in the dutch oven for a smoother result. Once it's chilled, transfer to air tight containers.

Yogurt lasts about two weeks in the refrigerator. I prefer to drain the whey out of yogurt through a double layer of cheesecloth in a strainer for 3-5 hours, depending on the desired thickness. Use a small wire whisk to smooth out the consistency before pouring into containers.

I freeze some of the whey to add to soup stocks. I hear it's good for pickling vegetables, too, but as of this writing, I haven't tried it.

Ghee

Ghee, an East Indian style clarified butter, is a good substitute for regular butter or margarine. Ghee is a bit different from the French clarified butter; it is cooked longer and the milk solids can be browned in the cooking, giving it a light, nutty flavor.

In the process of making ghee, all the water is boiled off and the milk solids are removed by straining. It will not become rancid, it is salt free and lactose and protein free. It does not burn or smoke. It does not need refrigeration, but I refrigerate it in hot weather to keep it from melting.

Ghee is said to be a gift of God - known for millennia as Liquid Gold. Ghee can be flavored, "browned" on purpose like butter for nuttiness or used as medicinal medium - there are many resources for such recipes.

2 pounds unsalted butter
I large heavy bottomed pot, not aluminum

Place butter in a large pot and set the burner on low.

The butter will be light and frothy as it begins to bubble and will crackle and pop as the moisture is evaporated.

Simmer the butter on low heat through two foaming – one to release the liquid, the second when the milk solids begin to separate and fall to the bottom of the pot. This will take

45 minutes to 2 hours, depending upon your stove. The pot must have high enough sides to handle the expansion during the foaming periods.

When the foaming stops and the milk solids have dropped to the bottom and are a lovely caramel brown, turn off the heat and let the ghee stand for about an hour, or until cool enough to pour through the cheesecloth into sterilized glass jars.

The darker brown the color, the more intense and nutty the flavor of the ghee. Keep watch, because seriously burned or blackened ghee is pretty irredeemable. This happened to me - I valiantly called it Ghee Noir, but it didn't taste very good.

Some people use the toasted milk solids to flavor food, but I toss it.

Makes about two pints.

Butter

On my grandfather's farm, we reserved about a gallon of cream a week for butter, putting 1 quart at a time into a bowl for mixing. A churn slowly agitates cream causing it to thicken and then break into butter particles, leaving buttermilk behind. A mixer is a little on the wild side and must be used carefully and slowly, so not to mix too much of the buttermilk into the butter. It also tends to splatter on faces and clothes... so cover the bowl and mixer with a dish towel.

The butter particles will gather together. Remove it from the bowl in a lump, set aside the buttermilk. Squeeze the remaining buttermilk out of the butter. Work it in your hands, and rinse in lukewarm water. Keep pressing the clear water out with hands or a paddle.

While kneading, you can add canning salt, about 1 teaspoon per pound of butter. I have used kosher salt. Or leave it unsalted.

After forming the butter into balls or pressing into molds, wrap it in parchment paper for refrigerating or freezing.

FRUIT, JAMS & SPREADS

APPLE SAUCE

Apples
Cinnamon

For canning you'll need:
Jar grabber (to pick up the hot jars)
Lid lifter
Small funnel
1 large pot heavy-bottomed pot
Wooden spoons and ladles
Ball jars, including the lids and rings
1 Water Bath Canner (a huge pot with a lifting rack to sanitize the jars of applesauce after filling)

Choose sweet, almost over the hill apples. Ask for seconds, or culls, the smaller, misshapen apples. They're a bit cheaper.

One Bushel of apples = about 13 quarts of apple sauce.

Wash jars and lids

Wash and chop apples. Cook apples in about one inch of water in a heavy-bottomed pot. Cook until apples are soft. Add cinnamon. Save any juice to drink and then put your applesauce through a sieve. Place in clean jars and process in a water bath for about fifteen minutes.

APPLE BUTTER

9 quarts of Applesauce, fresh or canned (see above)
2 tablespoons of ground cinnamon
1 teaspoon ground cloves
1/2 teaspoon allspice
2 to 4 cups sugar or Stevia (Sugar is optional)

1 crockpot (slow cooker) 6 quart size (if your crockpot is smaller, just reduce the ingredients proportionately)

Large spoons and ladles

1 canner or a huge pot to sanitize the jars of apple butter after filling
Ball jars

See instructions below.

APRICOT JAM

8 cups chopped apricots
1/4 cup lemon juice
6 cups sugar
5 pint canning jars or
10 half-pints, with lids

Sterilize jars by boiling for 10 minutes in a hot water canner.

Combine all ingredients in a large stockpot. Bring to boil over medium high heat, stirring occasionally until the sugar dissolves.

Once mixture reaches a good boil, simmer for 30 minutes, stirring often to prevent sticking. Remove from heat and fill jars, leaving 1/4 inch space at the top.

Wipe rims of jars clean and put lids in place. Process in boiling water for 10 minutes.

APRICOT FRUIT LEATHER

2 cups apricots
1 Tablespoon lemon juice
2 Tablespoons honey

Cut apricots in half and remove pits. Blend smooth in a food processor or blender. Add honey and lemon juice and blend again. For most intense flavor, cook the apricots for 30 minutes, *then* blend and let cool before the next step.

Prepare a baking sheet with plastic wrap covering the bottom. Pour the mix onto the plastic wrap and smooth with a spatula. It should be about 1/8 inch thick.

The trays can be placed outside in the sun covered with a screen or cheesecloth (not touching the mixture) or placed in a 140° oven overnight. When dry, roll up in its plastic wrap and store in refrigerator or freezer.

APRICOT BREAD

1 cup apricots, pitted and chopped
1 cup sugar
2 Tablespoons butter, softened
1 egg
3/4 cup orange juice
2 cups all-purpose flour
2 teaspoons baking powder
1/4 teaspoon baking soda
1 teaspoon salt

In a mixing bowl, cream the sugar, butter and egg. Stir in orange juice. Combine flour, baking powder, baking soda and salt; stir into creamed mixture until just combined. Add apricots to batter. Pour into a greased loaf pan.

Bake at 350° for approximately 50 minutes or until a crack appears along the top. Cool a few minutes in pan before removing to a wire rack.

APRICOT PIE

4 cups sliced fresh apricots
1 cup sugar
1/3 cup flour
pinch ground nutmeg
1 Tablespoon lemon juice
1 pastry recipe, page 104, for double-crust 9-inch pie
milk
additional sugar

In a large bowl, toss apricots, sugar, flour and nutmeg. Sprinkle with lemon juice; mix well. Roll out half the dough and line a 9-inch pie plate; add filling. Roll out remaining pastry; place over filling; seal and flute edges. Brush with milk and sprinkle with sugar. Cover edges of pastry loosely with foil. Bake at 375° for 45 minutes or until golden brown.

LEMON CURD

3 large lemons
1/2 cup butter
1½ cups sugar
3 egg yolks, beaten

Wash the lemons and zest the rinds. Squeeze the lemons and strain the juice into the top of a double boiler. Add the zested peel, butter, sugar and egg yolks. Cook, stirring constantly, until the butter melts, the sugar dissolves and the curd begins to thicken, about five minutes. Don't let it boil – this will curdle the eggs. When the Lemon Curd is thick and creamy, immediately pour into a clean glass jar. Cover the curd with a towel or plastic wrap to keep a skin from forming, let cool, and then refrigerate. Curd will last in refrigerator about three weeks. This makes about three cups.

Author's Note: Meyer Lemons make a delicious Curd. They have thinner, more orangey skins, a cross between a lemon and a tangerine.

Brandied Fruit

2 firm peaches, slices
4 firm apricots, slices
2 apples, peeled and slices
2 pears, slices
6 prunes or plums, slices
1/2 cup raisins
1/2 cup brown sugar
1/4 cup brandy

Combine all ingredients in a heat proof bowl.

Bake, uncovered at 325° until bubbling—about twenty minutes. Serve warm with yogurt, sour cream or cream or ice cream.

Cranberry Orange Preserves

2 cups dried cherries
1 cup fresh cranberries
3 cups brown sugar
3/4 cup crystallized ginger, chopped
4 cups oranges, seeded and chopped (rind and all)
2 tablespoons lemon zest

Combine all ingredients in heavy saucepan with about ½ cup water. Bring to boil. Reduce to simmer and cook about 8 minutes, stirring occasionally.

When cranberries begin to pop, remove from heat. Cool. Spoon into jars. Keep refrigerated.

TOMATOES

OVEN DRIED ROMA TOMATOES

30 firm but ripe Roma tomatoes
Olive oil
About a teaspoon each of thyme,
rosemary & oregano
Kosher Salt

Slice tomatoes in half lengthwise. Place cut side up on 2 parchment covered sheet pans. Drizzle liberally with olive oil. Sprinkle with salt and herbs. Place in 200° oven for 5-8 hours, depending upon the degree of dryness desired. The idea is to simply dry out the juices. If you go too far, the tomatoes get leathery. The perfect dried tomato will have a consistency much like sun-dried tomatoes.

There are so many uses for Oven Roasted Tomatoes, but two favorites come to mind: Chopped up warm and served over pasta with Parmesan Cheese or as an accompaniment to Citrus Cured Salmon, page 80.

TOMATO PASTE

Peel and seed Roma tomatoes, and then roughly chop them into small pieces to help get the breaking-down process started. You can actually leave the seeds and skin on for an even deeper tomato flavor if you like, but you'll need a food mill to sieve them out later.

Put the tomatoes in a medium-sized sauce pan over low heat. The tomatoes should cover the bottom of the pan by about an inch - not too full, then add a small amount of salt.

Cook the tomatoes uncovered, stirring every so often, until they've reached a thick, paste-like consistency. Lower the heat further if necessary. You should see steam coming off the tomatoes, but they shouldn't really be bubbling. Also, if the tomatoes don't look like they're breaking down evenly, run them in a food processor while they're still at a sauce-like consistency.

I freeze tomato paste in conveniently sized ice cube trays. When frozen, transfer to Ziplocs.

Flossie's Spaghetti Sauce

25 ripe but firm Roma tomatoes, chopped
4 Tablespoons olive oil
1 onion, chopped
2 carrots, chopped
2 stalks celery
4 cloves garlic, minced
1/4 cup chopped fresh basil
1/4 teaspoon Italian seasoning
1/4 cup burgundy or other full-bodied red wine
1 bay leaf
2 Tablespoons tomato paste

Cook onion, carrot, celery and garlic in oil until onion softens, about 5 minutes. Stir in chopped tomato, basil, Italian seasoning, wine and bay leaf. Cover and simmer 2 hours.

Stir in tomato paste and simmer an additional 2 hours.

Discard bay leaf and serve over cooked pasta or spaghetti squash.

Warm Tomato Chutney

six large Roma tomatoes, quartered
2 Tablespoons olive oil
1/4 yellow onion, chopped
1 Tablespoon cumin seeds
2 teaspoons brown mustard seeds
2 Tablespoons Balsamic vinegar
2 Tablespoons brown sugar
salt and pepper to taste

Sauté tomatoes and onion in hot olive oil with the cumin and mustard seeds. Cook until seeds pop and onions and tomatoes are softened. Add vinegar and brown sugar and cook until the moisture is absorbed, about five minutes. Serve warm or room temperature.

Tomato Basil Bisque

4 pounds ripe plum tomatoes, cut in half lengthwise
1/4 cup plus 2 tablespoons olive oil
2 tablespoons unsalted butter
1/4 teaspoon crushed red pepper flakes
1 tablespoon kosher salt
1½ teaspoons freshly ground black pepper
2 chopped yellow onions (about two cups)
6 garlic cloves, minced
4 cups fresh basil leaves, packed
1 teaspoon fresh thyme leaves
1 quart chicken stock or water

Preheat the oven to 400°. Toss together the tomatoes, 1/4 cup olive oil, salt, and pepper. Spread the tomatoes in 1 layer on a baking sheet and roast for 45 minutes.

In an 8-quart stockpot over medium heat, sauté the onions and garlic with 2 tablespoons of olive oil, the butter, and red pepper flakes for 10 minutes, until the onions start to brown. Add the tomatoes (including liquid), basil, thyme, and chicken stock. Simmer uncovered for 40 minutes. Pass through a food mill with the coarse blade. Taste for seasonings. Serve hot or cold.

KETCHUP

4 cups fresh chopped Roma tomatoes
1/2 cup water
2/3 cup white sugar
(or maple syrup or sucanat)
3/4 cup distilled white vinegar
1 teaspoon finely minced white onion
1 clove garlic, finely minced (or juiced)
1 teaspoon salt
1/8 teaspoon celery salt
1/8 teaspoon hot mustard powder
1/4 teaspoon finely ground black pepper
1 whole clove

Place chopped tomatoes into slow cooker.

Add sugar, vinegar, onion powder, garlic powder, salt, celery salt, mustard powder, black pepper, cayenne pepper, and whole clove; whisk to combine.

Cook on low, uncovered, until mixture is reduced by half and very thick, 10 to 12 hours. Stir every hour or so.

Smooth the texture of the ketchup using an immersion blender, about 20 seconds. Ladle the ketchup into a fine strainer and press mixture with the back of a ladle to strain out any skins and seeds. Transfer the strained ketchup to a bowl. Cool completely before tasting to adjust salt, black pepper, or cayenne pepper. Refrigerate.

TOMATO SALSA

6 ripe red tomatoes, chopped
1 red or 6 green onions, chopped
Jalapeno chilies to taste, finely chopped
Juice of 1/2 lemon
Cilantro to taste, chopped (optional)
salt and pepper to taste

Combine ingredients in a bowl and refrigerate until use. Will hold in refrigerator several days.

MANGO (OR PAPAYA OR PEACH) SALSA

To above recipe, add a chopped mango, papaya and/or 2 peaches

Oils, Vinegars & Dressings

Infused Oils

Quickie Version:

Make an infused oil by mixing a spice or powder in a glass jar with enough water to make a paste. Add a mild flavored oil (regular not extra virgin olive oil, or grape seed or safflower). Cap and shake the jar to distribute. Let stand for a few days. The residue sinks to the bottom. Pour or skim off oil. Use in sautéing, in vinaigrettes, sauces or marinades, sprinkle on salads.

Not So Quickie Version:

Bring a quart or more of oil to simmer - do not boil, or you will crisp the herbs. Remove the oil from heat. Toss in a handful of fresh or dried herbs or spices of choice.* Let stand twenty minutes to steep. Place a sprig of dried herbs in clean bottles. Strain infused oil into bottles.

For herbal infusions, used dried herbs.

*Possible spices: paprika, wasabi, chili, ginger, mustard, cardamom, nutmeg, cinnamon, saffron, clove, cumin.

*Possible herbs: tarragon, rosemary, sage, fennel, oregano, bay. Use whole herbs when possible.

Making fresh dressings is so easy and soooo much tastier than bottled. Keep in a lovely bottle dedicated to your special homemade dressings.

CREAMY TOFU DRESSING

2 inch piece firm tofu
1 Tablespoon honey
1 Tablespoon Bragg's Liquid Aminos or Soy Sauce
1 Tablespoon lemon juice
1/2 cup orange juice

MISO DRESSING

1 Tablespoon white miso paste
1 Tablespoon honey
1 Tablespoon Bragg's Liquid Aminos or Soy Sauce
1 Tablespoon Lemon juice
1 Tablespoon orange juice

LEMON-LIME DRESSING

1 Tablespoon olive oil
1 Tablespoon honey
1 Tablespoon Bragg's Liquid Aminos or Soy Sauce
1 Tablespoon lemon juice
3/4 cup lime juice

MINTED CITRUS DRESSING

Juice of four lemons
Juice of two oranges
2 Tablespoons honey, Sucanat or sugar
3 Tablespoons Bragg's Liquid Aminos or Soy Sauce
1 Tablespoon olive oil
2 Tablespoons crushed dried mint or
1 Tablespoon chopped fresh mint

Dijon Mustard Dressing

2 Tablespoons Dijon mustard
1 Tablespoon olive oil
1 Tablespoon honey
1 Tablespoon Bragg's Liquid Aminos or Soy Sauce
1 Tablespoon lemon juice
1/2 cup orange juice

Balsamic Dressing

2 Tablespoons Dijon mustard
1 Tablespoon olive oil
1 Tablespoon honey
1 Tablespoon Bragg's Liquid Aminos or Soy Sauce
1 Tablespoon balsamic vinegar
1/2 cup orange juice

Poppy seed Dressing

1 Tablespoon Dijon mustard
1 Tablespoon olive oil
1 Tablespoon honey
1 Tablespoon Bragg's Liquid Aminos or Soy Sauce
1 Tablespoon lemon juice
1/2 cup orange juice
1/4 cup yogurt
1 Tablespoon poppy seeds

Yogurt Dill Dressing

1 Tablespoon olive oil
1 Tablespoon honey
1 Tablespoon Bragg's Liquid Aminos or Soy Sauce
1 Tablespoon lemon juice
1/2 cup orange juice
1/4 cup yogurt
2 Tablespoons minced fresh dill

Cilantro Dressing

1/2 cup cilantro
1/4 cup olive oil
1 Tablespoon lime juice
1 clove finely minced garlic
pinch of Mexican oregano
salt to taste

Combine and blend all ingredients in a blender or food processor.

French Vinaigrette

1/8 teaspoon sea salt
1 Tablespoon sherry wine vinegar
1/2 small shallot, peeled and minced
1/2 teaspoon Dijon mustard
4 Tablespoons olive oil

In a small jar, mix together the salt, vinegar, and shallot. Let stand for about ten minutes.

Mix in the Dijon mustard, add olive oil. Shake well.

GREEN GODDESS DRESSING

George Arliss (1868-1946), a prominent English stage star, was staying at The Palace Hotel in San Francisco in 1923 during the run of a play called "The Green Goddess" (by William Archer). In preparing for a banquet in Mr. Arliss's honor, the Executive Chef of the hotel used an array of chopped green herbs to suggest the name of the play. Green Goddess Dressing became the hotel's signature salad dressing and has been served in the hotel's Garden Court Restaurant since that time. Goes well with seafood salads, particularly crab.

The original recipe:
1 garlic clove
2 cups of mayonnaise
4 minced anchovy fillets
1 green onion, chopped
2 teaspoons chopped parsley
2 teaspoons chopped chives
1 Tablespoon tarragon vinegar (or to taste)
1/4 teaspoon dried or 1 teaspoon cut, fresh tarragon

Toss ingredients in food processor and give it a whirl! Pour over salad greens, watercress, or seafood salad.

Curing & Pickling
Citrus Cured Salmon

This recipe takes 24-48 hours to cure the salmon. The longer it cures, the dryer it gets. It's easy. Watch your knuckles, though. I invariably grate some into the citrus zest. Sorry.

5 pounds fresh center-cut Salmon
in approximately one pound pieces, skin on

remove pin bones (with a pair of pliers dedicated
to this activity)

approximately:
three pounds rock salt
three pounds sugar
three cups mixed zest of lemons, oranges & limes

Mix the zest, salt and sugar in a large bowl. Using two glass 9 x 12 inch pans, lay large pieces of plastic wrap, enough to completely wrap around the fish, into the pans. Spread 1/4 of the salt-sugar-zest mixture evenly into the bottom of each the pan. Lay the pieces of salmon, skin side down, onto the mixture. Spread the remaining mixture over the top of the salmon. Wrap tightly with the plastic wrap, and then wrap with foil. Place in refrigerator with weights on top. Turn every twelve hours, replacing the weights each time, for at least 24 hours.

I started this cure on Monday afternoon. On Tuesday morning, I turned it, on Tuesday evening I turned it. On Wednesday morning, I took it out of its wrapping, and washed off the mixture with cold water and patted it dry with paper towels. It's sad to see all those Omega 3s washed away with the fish oil, but, oh well.

When serving, slice (skin-side down) very, very thinly, on the diagonal, avoiding the skin at the bottom of your slice, and arrange in little curls on a platter.

Citrus Cured Salmon freezes well.

MEYER LEMON PRESERVES

Moroccan, Russian, Indian, African... who knows who first made this up. Ibn Battuta, considered one of the greatest travelers of all time, ate preserved lemons in Somalia in 1325!

Meyer lemons
 (enough to fill your jar)
salt
spices *(see below)*
lemon juice

Slice the washed lemons lengthwise in quarters or slivers. Place in large mixing bowl. Have clean glass jars available. Toss lemons in Kosher or sea salt, using about one Tablespoon per lemon. Toss in several cinnamon sticks, sprinkle with cumin seeds, peppercorns and a bay leaf or two. Toss well to distribute all spices.

Fill clean glass jars with lemon mixture. Pour in lemon juice to cover all lemons. Seal the jars in a hot water bath (water at a simmer) for 10 minutes. Not totally necessary if the lemons are refrigerated, but be safe.

Every few days for three weeks, turn jar(s) upside down and then right side up. Keep refrigerated.

Use on vegetable or meat dishes, as salad topping, in sandwiches. Use as part of a *Gremolata* (lemon, parsley, fresh garlic).

CORNICHONS

6 pounds (about 40) tiny fresh picked cucumbers, 1-2 inches long each
1½ cups coarse (kosher) salt or 1 ¼ cups pickling salt
1/4 cup white wine vinegar or distilled white vinegar
18 sprigs fresh tarragon
6 shallots, peeled and sliced thin
1 tablespoon mustard seed
1 tablespoon black peppercorns
2 quarts white wine vinegar, more if needed

Wash cucumbers in cold water and remove any blossoms. Rinse and drain. Mix with salt in stainless steel or ceramic bowl. Cover the bowl with a cloth and let stand at room temperature for 24 hours. Stir to keep the developing brine well mixed. Next day, drain the cucumbers and rinse in 3 quarts of cold water and ¼ cup white wine vinegar or distilled white vinegar. Let stand 15 minutes. And let dry.

Scald and drain a 1 gallon crock. Approximate your layers and divide ingredients into that number. Layer: Tarragon, cucumbers, spices. Repeat until crock is filled about 2/3 of the way. Pour in enough white wine or distilled vinegar to cover the cucumbers and seasonings by 2 inches.

Cover the crock with a plate on which you set a brick or heavy weight. Leave the pickles in a cool, dark spot for a month, after which they will be ready to use.

Bread and Butter Pickles

Makes about ten 12 oz. jars of pickles

15 cups sliced pickling cucumbers
3 onions, thinly sliced
1/4 cup coarse salt
4 cups crushed ice
2½ cups apple cider vinegar
2 cups sugar
3/4 teaspoon turmeric
1/2 teaspoon celery seed
1 Tablespoon brown mustard seeds

Combine cucumbers, onions, salt and ice in a large bowl. Mix well. Put a weight on it (a plate with a brick works well) and allow to stand 5 hours. Drain thoroughly.

Combine vinegar, sugar, turmeric, celery seed and brown mustard seed in a large pot. Add drained cucumbers.

Place pot on medium low heat. Bring almost to a boil, but DO NOT ALLOW TO BOIL.

Remove from heat. Seal in sterilized jars, 10 minutes in a hot water bath. To sterilize jars: Wash them well in hot soapy water and dry them off. Place on a cookie sheet, right side up, at 225°F for 15 minutes. Turn off oven and leave them in there until you need them.

If you increase the spices and add some grated ginger, these are quite sparkly with Indian food.

PICKLED GRAPES

1/2 cup vinegar
   (use white wine vinegar for green grapes,
   red wine vinegar for red grapes)
1/2 cup water
1 bunch fresh or 1 Tablespoon dried tarragon
4-5 crushed coriander seeds
1/2 teaspoon crushed cumin seeds
1 crumbled bay leaf
1 clove garlic, crushed
1 cup seedless grapes

Combine first seven ingredients. Toss with grapes. Place in glass or plastic container.

Cover and refrigerate 24 hours.

Can be doubled, tripled, quadrupled…

Serve with grilled or roasted meats.

ZUCCHINI PICKLES

2 pounds zucchini, thinly sliced
1/2 pound onions, quartered and thinly sliced
1/4 cup salt
2 cups white sugar
2 cups apple cider vinegar
1 teaspoon celery seed
1 teaspoon ground turmeric
1 teaspoon prepared yellow mustard
2 teaspoons mustard seeds
3 1-quart canning jars with lids and rings

Place zucchini, onions and salt into a large bowl, cover with water, and stir until salt is dissolved. Let the zucchini soak in the salted water for 2 hours; drain and transfer to a large heat proof bowl.

Bring sugar, vinegar, celery seed, turmeric, mustard, and mustard seeds to a boil in a saucepan; pour the mixture over the zucchini and onions. Let the mixture stand for 2 more hours. Return zucchini, onions, and pickling liquid with spices to a large pot and bring to a boil. Boil for 3 minutes.

While vegetables are soaking in pickling liquid, sterilize jars and lids in boiling water for at least 5 minutes.

Pack the zucchini and onion into the hot, sterilized jars, filling the jars to within ¼ inch of the top with pickling liquid.

Run a knife or a thin spatula around the insides of the jars after they have been filled to remove any air bubbles.

Wipe the rims of the jars with a moist paper towel to remove any food residue. Top with lids and screw on rings.

Place a rack in the bottom of a large stockpot and fill halfway with water. Bring to a boil and lower jars into the boiling water using a holder. Leave a 2-inch space between the jars. Pour in more boiling water if necessary to bring the water level to at least 1 inch above the tops of the jars.

Bring the water to a rolling boil, cover the pot, and process for 10 minutes.

Remove the jars from the stockpot and place onto a cloth-covered or wood surface, several inches apart, until cool.

Once cool, press the top of each lid with a finger, ensuring that the seal is tight (lid does not move up or down at all). Store in a cool, dark area, and wait at least 24 hours before opening.

About Freezing

Use only fruits and veggies in excellent condition that have been thoroughly cleaned. Most vegetables you plan to freeze should be blanched for two to five minutes.

Blanching—the process of heating vegetables with boiling water or steam for a set amount of time, then immediately plunging them into cold or iced water—stops enzyme activity that causes vegetables to lose nutrients and change texture. The cooled veggies can then be packed into bags, jars or other freezer-safe storage containers.

Fruits or blanched vegetables can also be patted dry with clean kitchen towels, frozen in a single layer on cookie sheets, and then put into containers. Using cookie sheets for freezing ensures that the fruits and vegetables won't all stick together, thus allowing you to remove a handful at a time from the container.

Unless you're freezing liquids—which require space for expansion—you should remove as much air as possible from within the freezer container. With zip-close freezer bags, you must squeeze out the air by hand, whereas a vacuum sealer will suck out air as it seals the bags. Vacuum sealing reduces freezer burn (the formation of ice crystals that refreeze around the edges of the food and damage its taste and texture) because the crystals have no space in which to form.

Condiments & Sauces

Vanilla Extract

Buy Fair Trade vanilla beans whenever possible (Mountain Rose Herbs is my first choice). Grade B is fine for extract, although Grade A is good for cooking.

As to alcohol, Vodka has the most neutral flavor, but bourbon, brandy, or rum are interesting. Experiment for unique flavors. An inexpensive 40% (80 proof) alcohol works well. Infuse vanilla beans in alcohol for a minimum of one month and as long as two months. Flavors become more interesting and complex over time, like wine.

3 vanilla beans
8 ounces alcohol
Cutting board and knife
Clean jar or bottle
New bottle(s) for packaging (optional)
Small funnel (optional)
Coffee filter (optional)

Split each vanilla bean in half lengthwise, but don't split it apart. If you like, you can leave an inch connected at the end of the bean for an attractive presentation. You can also chop the beans into smaller pieces if necessary to fit in your jar or bottle. I like using whole, partially split beans.

Place the vanilla beans in a clean jar or bottle. Cover them with alcohol, making sure they are completely submerged. Cap the jar or bottle and give it a good shake.

Store the jar or bottle of vanilla beans in a cool, dark place for at least one month, shaking it now and then. Taste the extract and let it infuse longer for a stronger flavor.

You can remove the vanilla pods and decant the extract into a pretty bottle. The little flecks of seeds are nice, but if you want a clear extract , strain them out using a coffee filter.

You can also leave the beans in the alcohol and top off the bottle as you use it.

For Vanilla Sugar

Bake the vanilla bean pod, with beans intact, at 150 degrees for 20 minutes, until they're dry and brittle.

Cool and grind until fine. Push through a sieve to remove large pieces and stir into sugar.

Use one Tablespoon of vanilla to one pound of sugar.

Marie Gillan's Mustard

From Marie's family, to mine, to yours, this mustard will delight the palate

1 two ounce can Coleman's or other hot mustard powder
1 cup sugar or other sweetener
(I prefer maple syrup these days, or even Stevia, which isn't sweet at all but an herb that tricks your tongue to sweetness)
1 cup malt vinegar

Mix the three ingredients together in the top of a double boiler, cover and let stand over night.

Add three beaten eggs. Cook over water until thickened - about ten minutes. Let cool. Pour into a jar. Use it on anything. Everything.

Aioli

2 egg yolks
1/8 teaspoon sea salt
1 cup virgin olive oil
Juice of 1/2 lemon
1/2 teaspoon cold water

Turn on food processor and slowly add egg yolks. Add in half of the olive oil, continuing to pulse the food processor slowly so the oil will emulsify and thicken your sauce. Once the first half of the oil is incorporated, add the water and the lemon juice. Slowly add the rest of the oil. The mixture thickens as you continue to blend.

Fresh Garlic Aioli

4 garlic cloves, peeled, chopped fine
1/8 teaspoon sea salt
2 egg yolks
1 cup virgin olive oil
Juice of 1/2 lemon
1/2 teaspoon cold water

Chop up the garlic and salt in the food processor and slowly add the egg yolks. Add in half of the continuing to pulse the food processor slowly so the oil will emulsify and thicken your sauce.

Once the first half of the oil is incorporated, add the water and the lemon juice. Slowly add the rest of the oil. The mixture thickens as you continue to blend.

Hollandaise

3 egg yolks
1 teaspoon water
1/4 teaspoon sugar
1½ sticks unsalted butter, chilled and chopped
1/2 teaspoon kosher salt
2 teaspoons fresh lemon juice
1/8 teaspoon cayenne pepper

Pour 1-inch of water into a large saucepan; over medium heat, bring to a simmer. Once simmering, reduce the heat to low.

Place egg yolks and 1 teaspoon water in a medium mixing bowl and whisk until mixture lightens in color, 1 to 2 minutes. Add the sugar and whisk for another 30 seconds. Place the mixture over the simmering water and whisk constantly for 3 to 5 minutes, or until the mixture coats the back of a spoon.

Remove the bowl from over the pan and gradually add the butter, 1 piece at a time, and whisk until all of the butter is incorporated. Place the bowl back over the simmering water occasionally so that it will be warm enough the melt the butter. Add the salt, lemon juice, and cayenne pepper. Serve immediately or keep warm until used.

CARAMEL SAUCE

1 1/4 cups heavy cream
1 teaspoon vanilla extract
1 1/2 cups granulated sugar
1/3 cup water
1/2 teaspoon lemon juice
1/2 teaspoon kosher salt, plus more as needed

Combine cream and vanilla, set aside.

Add sugar and water to a very clean medium heavy bottomed saucepan. Gently stir so that the sugar is just moistened by the water. Cook the sugar, water and lemon juice over low heat until the sugar dissolves and the mixture is clear, about 10 minutes. Do not stir while the sugar cooks.

Cover the pot with a lid for one minute. (This adds steam to the pot and washes any sugar clinging to the sides of the pan down into the sugar syrup, preventing crystallization).

Remove lid and attach a very clean candy thermometer to the side of the pan. Increase heat to medium and cook, without stirring, until the sugar reaches 350° F, 5 to 10 minutes.

(Gently tilt the saucepan from side-to-side to distribute any hot spots, but do not use a spoon).

Once the caramel reaches 350° F, remove the pan from the heat and slowly pour in the vanilla cream. The caramel *will* splatter and bubble, so be careful during this step. If the caramel hardens, it will melt back into a smooth caramel in a minute.

Place the caramel back onto the burner over low heat and cook for 2 minutes, constantly stirring until the solids have dissolved and the caramel is smooth.

Stir in the ½ teaspoon of salt then cool to room temperature. As the caramel cools, taste it to see if you need to add additional salt.

Cover tightly and keep in the refrigerator up to two weeks. Pours easily when warmed.

Caramel Sauce Tips:

DO use oven mitts when moving the pot around - it's HOT!

DON'T stir until the cream is added in the end - just gently tilt or swirl the pan from side-to-side to ensure everything cooks evenly.

DO use the lemon juice - it can help prevent crystallization.

Enchilada Sauce

8 dried Ancho chilies
two gallons boiling water
1/3 cup canola oil
4 cups each, chopped: carrots, onions, celery
2 -3 cloves garlic, chopped
about a gallon of veggie or chicken stock (pages 39-43)
1/2-1 cup cornmeal
1/4 cup brown sugar
1-2 teaspoons ground cumin
salt and pepper to taste
oregano to taste, optional

Place dried chilies in boiling water and turn off the heat. Soak about three hours or overnight. Drain, cool, stem and seed the chilies. Leave the skins on.

Sauté vegetables in hot oil in large pot until soft. Add chilies and stock. Simmer 20 minutes.

Blend with hand held soup blender. Thicken with cornmeal, season with brown sugar, cumin, salt and pepper.

This makes a lot. Can be frozen in Ziplocs or plastic containers.

Herbs, Pestos & Blends

Basil or Cilantro Pesto

2 bunches fresh basil or cilantro
1 bunch scallions
1/2 cup pine nuts
squeeze of lemon
dash of salt
1/2 cup Parmesan (for basil pesto only)

Place all ingredient in food processor and whirl until a gritty-looking paste. Scoop by teaspoon into clean ice trays. Freeze overnight. Transfer Pesto Cubes to a Ziploc bag, label and keep in freezer.

Ancho Chili Powder

Find or grow Ancho Chilies! Make sure they are dry and brick red. Grind them to a powder. Amazing Chili Powder.

Curry Blend

In India, curry means sauce, or gravy. However, this is my personal blend for a good combination of Eastern spices.

4 Tablespoons cumin seeds
4 Tablespoons coriander seeds
4 teaspoons ground turmeric
1 teaspoon crushed red pepper flakes
1 teaspoon brown mustard seeds
1 teaspoon ground ginger

Pulse in food processor. I use a coffee grinder dedicated to grinding spices - and, I like a coarse grind, but you can make it a fine powder, too.

Use less red pepper chili flakes for a milder curry blend.

Cereals

Toasted Oat and Coconut Muesli

4 cups old-fashioned rolled oats
1 cup unsweetened coconut
1 cup coarsely chopped dry roasted almonds
1 cup dried cranberries or other dried fruit
1 cup chopped candied ginger
1/2 teaspoon ground cinnamon
1/4 teaspoon freshly grated nutmeg
1/2 teaspoon salt
Almond milk
Maple syrup

Place two racks in the center and upper third of the oven. Preheat oven to 325°. Mix together oats and coconut on un-greased and unlined baking sheets. Toast until coconut is golden brown, 5 to 7 minutes. Coconut browns quickly, keep an eye on it. Remove from the oven and cool.

In a large bowl toss together oats & coconut, dried cranberries, spices and salt. Stores in airtight jars or Ziplocs.

Prepare muesli a few hours before you'd like to serve it: pour almond milk over the muesli, cover and refrigerate for at least 2 hours.

When ready to serve, drizzle with maple syrup.

Great Granola
Fruit sugars only • low fat

2 cups organic rolled oats
1/4 cup sesame seeds
1/4 cup nuts, such as almonds, walnuts or pine nuts
1/4 cup sunflower seeds
2 Tablespoons cinnamon
1 Tablespoon cardamom
1/2 teaspoon salt, optional
2 Tablespoons grated orange peel
1/2 cup apple or orange juice concentrate, thawed
1/2 cup date pieces
1/2 cup raisins or currants
1/2 cup mixed dried fruit pieces
1/2 cup coconut, optional

Pre-heat oven to 325°

In a large mixing bowl, combine the oats, seeds, nuts, spices and orange peel. Add the juice concentrate and mix well with large wooden spoon.

Spread mixture on parchment covered baking sheets. Bake for about 45 minutes or until lightly toasted and dry.

Cool before adding fruits and optional coconut.

GRANOLA BARS

1 cup oats or puffed rice
1 cup shredded coconut
1/4 cup sunflower seeds
1/4 cup sesame seeds
1 teaspoon orange peel or zest
1/2 cup raw sugar
1/2 can apple juice concentrate
1/4cup hot water

Mix together in large bowl. Spread out on sheet pan and lightly toast for about ten minutes at 300°. Toss with:

1/2 cup currants or raisins*
1/2 cup date pieces
1/4 cup maple syrup

Press mixture into prepared pan. Bake fifteen minutes at 325°. Cool slightly before cutting. Store in airtight container.

*or cranberries, blueberries, apricots….

Breads, Pastas and Baking

Oatmeal Bread

2 large or 4 small loaves
Baking spray

2 cups oatmeal, either rolled or steel cut
4 cups boiling water
8 oz. Dark molasses
2 tablespoons melted butter
1 cup dry milk
3 tablespoons yeast
1 teaspoon salt
4 cups wheat flour
4 cups white flour

Place oatmeal in large mixing bowl, pour boiling water over and stir. Let cool for about two hours or overnight. Dissolve yeast in 1/4 cup lukewarm water. To oatmeal, add molasses, melted butter, dry milk, dissolved yeast. Mix well. Let stand fifteen minutes. Add salt and begin adding flour, a little at a time, alternating between wheat and white to achieve a soft but firm dough. You may not need all eight cups flour.

Cover bowl and let rise for several hours, until doubled in bulk. Punch down and roll out onto floured board. Knead and shape into loaves.

Place dough into well sprayed baking pans and let rise again, until dough comes over top of pans. Preheat oven to 350°.

Bake for approximately 40 minutes. When inserted knife or skewer comes out clean, it's done!

(Cracked wheat or left over cooked oatmeal can also be used. If using cooked oatmeal, delete the 4 cups boiling water.)

BASIC PASTRY DOUGH

For one two-crust pie or two pies with a bottom crust and a crumble topping (page 117)

2½ cups pastry flour
1½ cups unsalted butter, cut in pieces
1/2 teaspoon salt
1/4 to 1/2 cup orange juice

Blend first four ingredients in food processor until butter is distributed and the mixture looks and feels like coarse meal. Slowly add orange juice through top of food processor until a ball of dough begins to form. Do not add too much juice or the dough will be too sticky.

Remove from processor, form into a ball, dust with flour, wrap in plastic and refrigerate for 1 hour or overnight.

Roll out onto floured board for pies, pasties or other pastry items.

Pizza Dough

1 cup lukewarm water
1 package active dry yeast
1 tablespoon sugar
2½ - 3 cups flour
2 tablespoons olive oil
1/2 teaspoon salt

Combine the water, yeast and sugar in a bowl. Let stand ten minutes. Add half the flour and stir well. Add the salt and the oil and enough of the remaining flour to form smooth, soft dough.

Turn out onto lightly floured board and knead five minutes. If the dough is too sticky, sprinkle with more flour while kneading.

Place dough in a lightly oiled bowl and let stand, covered, about 45 minutes. After the dough has risen, place on a lightly floured surface and divide into four pieces. Let stand, covered, 20 minutes.

Roll out mini pizzas and bake for Salad on Pizza, or top with sauce, fresh mozzarella cheese and other things of choice.

Bake in 375° oven for about 20 minutes.

FRENCH BREAD

2 tablespoons active dry yeast
2 tablespoons sugar
4 cups lukewarm water
8 cups sifted white flour
1 teaspoon salt

In a large bowl, dissolve the yeast and sugar in lukewarm water. Let stand for two minutes. Stir in half the flour and the salt. Add just enough of the remaining flour to hold the dough together—it will form soft, slightly sticky dough.

Knead in the bowl for about five minutes, adding just enough more flour to assist kneading and not stick to your hands. Cover and let rise until double, 1-2 hours. Set near a warm oven or fire to quicken the rising process.

Preheat the oven to 400°

When the dough has risen, punch it down with your hand and divide into loaves: two medium loaf pans, two baguette pans or one large loaf pan. A clay pan will produce a great crust. Let rise again for 1/2 hour to 45 minutes, or until the dough has risen over the top of the pan(s).

Bake for about forty minutes on the middle rack. Place trays of water on the rack below. The loaves will be brown and crusty when they are done. Pierce with skewer for doneness—if they come out clean, that's that! Cool for one hour before slicing.

Sourdough Starter

"Ew! What is that?" I asked my mother, noticing the burbling glop in the jar in the fridge.

"Sourdough Starter," she said, as she took it out, removed some of the glop from the jar, added some other stuff to it and put it back.

"Why did you do that?" I asked.

"You have to feed it," she said.

"Ew! It's alive?"

In a spring-top jar on the top shelf of the refrigerator was my mother's prized, seven year old Sourdough Starter, a wedding gift from a San Francisco girlfriend. Sourdough Starter: a creature that lived in the fridge that had to be fed once a week!

Sourdough likely originated around 1500 BC, in Egypt, and was the first form of leavening historically noted. Throughout the Middle Ages, Sourdough leavened most bread, then was replaced by the barm from beer brewing and then later cultured yeast.

The creature in the fridge is a batter of flour and water, filled with living yeast and bacteria, which form a stable symbiotic relationship, creating a little tribe of microorganisms, and, with proper care and feeding, and very short walks from fridge to counter and back to fridge, can live for eons. I named our Sourdough Starter Fred.

Blend a cup of warm water and a cup of flour, and pour it into a clean, wide-mouthed glass jar with a rubber seal: or a crock with a loose lid.

Plastic containers are OK, but not ideal. They're plastic. Metallic containers are chemically reactive and would probably turn your starter to some other science experiment (for the same reason, avoid using metal utensils to stir your starter).

You can add a little commercial yeast to a Starter to give it a boost and make it lighter, but sourdough snobs frown on this. And, Starter made with commercial yeast produces less distinctive sour flavor than the real thing.

Sourdough Starter has to be kept warm to propagate, so experienced miners and settlers in California carried a well-guarded pouch of starter either around their neck or on a belt inside their pants. Sourdough Bread became so common during the Northern California Gold Rush, that "Sourdough" became a general nickname for the gold prospectors, and "Sourdough Sam" still reigns supreme as the mascot of the San Francisco 49ers.

To make Sourdough Bread, remove some of the Starter from your container and blend it with some flour to make dough, always adding something back to the container. The yeast propagates, and leavens your bread in its own gaseous way.

For three or four days, keep your Fred in a warm place; 70-80°F, but no hotter than 100°! High temperature will kill your little budding blob. The yeast already in the flour will grow quickly under these conditions. To feed the Starter, discard half of it and add a half-cup of flour and a half-cup of water, every 24 hours.

It will form a liquid on top with a beery fragrance which is called Hooch, an alcoholic froth. Hooch, according to legend, is shortened from the Tlingit Hootchinoo, the name of an Alaskan indigenous tribe that distilled some kind of liquor. It is what makes sourdough sour dough! When the Hooch forms, you have achieved Sourdough Starter. Mix it back in.

Keep the starter in your fridge, with a loose lid on it - allow it to breath. Feed it once a week, or so. If you enjoy anthropomorphizing microorganisms, be sure to name your Creature.

Proofing the Sponge

Before you make dough, begin with a sponge, a fermented batter. Pour 2 cups of Sourdough Starter into a large glass or ceramic bowl. Warming the bowl for few minutes with hot water helps create the proper environment.

Add a cup of warm water and a cup of flour to the bowl. Stir well, and set it in a warm place for several hours. This is called "proofing," or fermenting. The longer you proof the sponge, the more sour the flavor.

The batter may be used for pancakes, waffles, muffins, bread or cake. The proofing-time varies, but setting your sponge out to proof overnight is great.

When using in a recipe, or for sharing with a friend, take 2 cups starter out and then add more flour and water to your Starter.

Sourdough Bread

2 cups of sponge from your proofed starter
3 cups of unbleached flour
2 tablespoons of oil (or softened butter)
4 teaspoons of sugar
2 teaspoons of salt

To the sponge, add the sugar, salt, and oil (the oil is optional - you can use softened butter instead, or no oil at all). Knead in flour about a half cup at a time to make nice, springy bread dough. Remember that flour amounts are approximate—when you get that bouncy "feel," stop adding flour.

Let the dough rise in a warm place, in a bowl covered loosely with a towel. Sourdough rises more slowly than yeast bread, about an hour or so. Let it double in bulk.

When it is soft and springy to the touch, punch the dough down and knead a little more. Make a loaf shape and place it on a baking sheet (lightly greased or sprinkled with cornmeal), or place in a sprayed loaf pan. Slit the top, if you like, cover the loaf with a towel and put it in a warm place to rise again, until doubled in bulk.

Place the pan with the loaf in your oven, turn your oven to 350° and bake the bread for 30-45 minutes. *Do not preheat the oven*. The loaf is done when the crust is brown and the bottom sounds hollow when thumped with your thumb. Turn the loaf out onto a cooling rack or a towel and let it cool for an hour before slicing.

POPOVERS

Preheat oven 375°
Popover pan or heavy muffin tin
Vegetable spray

6 eggs
1 Tablespoon vanilla
1/2 teaspoon salt
1¾ cups flour
2¾ cups milk (can be whole, 2% or fat free)
4 tablespoons butter, melted

Blend eggs, vanilla and salt in food processor. Add flour and milk alternately while food processor is whirling around. Add melted butter. Pour into pitcher. Cover. Best if refrigerated overnight to cure batter (the popovers will rise higher and pop better).

Heat popover pan or heavy muffin tin in oven for about fifteen minutes. Quickly remove from oven, spray heavily and pour cold batter to top of cups. Bake at 375° (without opening oven door) for about 40 minutes, until dark golden brown and firm to the touch.

Remove from oven and, using bamboo skewer, poke with many holes to allow the steam to escape (otherwise your popovers will collapse).

Serve with butter and jam or maple butter (1/2 softened butter and 1/2 maple syrup, blended in food processor).

Flatbread Crackers

3 cups flour
2 teaspoons baking powder
2 teaspoons salt
1 stick unsalted butter, cut in pieces
1 cup plain yogurt
1¼ cups sesame seeds, toasted

Glaze:
2 large eggs
2 Tablespoons sugar
1 Tablespoon Bragg's Liquid Aminos or soy sauce

In food processor, mix flour, baking powder and salt. Add butter and grind coarsely. Transfer to a large bowl and add yogurt and one cup of the sesame seeds. Mix to form a dough. Wrap in plastic and chill for 30 minutes.

Preheat oven to 325°

Stir eggs, sugar and Bragg's together. Set aside.

Divide the dough into quarters. Divide each quarter into 12 pieces. Rolling the dough, make 4 inch logs with your hands. Roll out each log with a floured rolling pin into a strip about 12 x 4 inches. Carefully transfer to a baking sheet covered with parchment. Brush strips with glaze and sprinkle with remaining seeds.

Bake crackers two sheets at a time, rotating upper and lower, 20 minutes max, until glaze is golden and crackers look crisp but not hard. Transfer to cooling rack and continue rolling and baking. Stores for about a week in airtight containers.

Chocolate Chip Cookies

2¼ cups all-purpose flour
1 teaspoon baking soda
1 teaspoon salt
1 cup (2 sticks) butter, softened
1/4 cup granulated sugar
1 cup packed brown sugar
1 teaspoon vanilla extract
2 large eggs
2 cups (12-oz. pkg.) mini semi-sweet chocolate morsels
1 cup chopped nuts (optional)

Preheat oven to 375°

Combine flour, baking soda and salt in small bowl. Beat butter, granulated sugar, brown sugar and vanilla extract in large mixer bowl until creamy. Add eggs, one at a time, beating well after each addition. Gradually beat in flour mixture. Stir in morsels and nuts. Drop by rounded tablespoon onto parchment lined baking sheets.

Bake for 9 to 11 minutes or until golden brown. Cool on baking sheets for 2 minutes; remove to wire racks to cool completely.

Pan Cookies:

Grease 15 x 10-inch jelly-roll pan. Prepare dough as above. Spread into prepared pan. Bake for 20 to 25 minutes or until golden brown. Cool in pan on wire rack. Makes 4 dozen bars.

Slice and Bake Cookies:

Prepare dough as above. Divide in half; wrap in waxed paper. Refrigerate for 1 hour or until firm.

Shape each half into 15-inch log; wrap in wax paper. Refrigerate for 30 more minutes.*

Preheat oven to 375° F. Cut logs into 1/2-inch-thick slices; place on un-greased baking sheets. Bake for 8 to 10 minutes or until golden brown.

Cool on baking sheets for 2 minutes; remove to wire racks to cool completely. Makes about 5 dozen cookies.

Dough may be stored in refrigerator for up to 1 week or in freezer for up to 8 weeks.

LEGENDARY CREAM SCONES

Preheat oven to 350°

3½ cups organic, unbleached pastry flour
3½ teaspoons baking powder
1/2 teaspoon salt
1 tablespoon bakers' superfine sugar

2 sticks 1 cup) unsalted butter, cut in pieces

4 eggs
2/3 cup heavy cream
2/3 cup sour cream

Sift dry ingredients. Beat eggs, cream and sour cream together in a separate bowl. Place dry ingredients and cold butter in food processor and process until mixture looks and feels like coarse meal, less than a minute. Add egg and cream mixture and flavor*; quickly mix together until dough forms a soft ball. Scoop out about one cup of dough for each scone onto sheet pan covered with parchment. Sprinkle with sugar (optional).

Bake about 20 minutes, or until golden and cooked through.

*2 Tablespoons lemon zest, dried fruit or savory herbs

Crumble Topping

2 cups flour
1 cup cold, unsalted butter
1 cup sugar
1 teaspoon cinnamon

Blend all ingredients in food processor until crumbly, less than a minute. (Do not over blend - will become too doughy.) Keep chilled or frozen. For savory topping, omit sugar and cinnamon and replace with herbs or cheese.

Doggie Cookies

parchment for baking
cookie cutter (dog bone shape is preferable, although any shape that makes you smile will do)

1 cup rolled oats
1/3 cup butter or oil
1½ cups chicken or veggie stock, brought to boil
3/4 cups cornmeal
1 teaspoon sugar
1 cup shredded cheddar cheese
1 egg, beaten
2-3 cups whole wheat flour

Preheat oven to 325°

Place parchment on baking sheet. In a large bowl, combine oats, butter or oil and stock. Let stand 10 minutes. Stir in next five ingredients. Add 2½ cups of flour, one cup at a time, mixing well after each addition. Turn onto floured board. Knead until no longer sticky, adding flour if necessary. Roll dough out onto floured board to ½ inch thickness. Cut with cookie cutter and place on sheet one inch apart. Bake 35-40 minutes or until light brown and dried out (to prevent moisture from turning them into a lovely penicillin blue). Cool completely before storing in an airtight container.

KITTY TREATS

parchment for baking
dough scraper

1 cup rolled oats
1/3 cup butter or oil
1½ cups fish stock, brought to boil
3/4 cup cornmeal
1 teaspoon sugar
1 cup shredded cheddar cheese
1 egg, beaten
2-3 cups whole wheat flour

Preheat oven to 325°

Place parchment on baking sheet. In a large bowl, combine oats, butter or oil and stock. Let stand 10 minutes. Stir in next five ingredients. Add 2 1/2 cups of flour, one cup at a time, mixing well after each addition. Turn onto floured board. Knead until no longer sticky, adding flour if necessary. Roll dough out onto floured board in long, thin snakes. Cut with dough scraper (like gnocchi) into little ½ bites and place on sheet. Bake 25 minutes or until light brown and dried out. Cool completely before storing in an airtight container.

PONY COOKIES

parchment for baking
12 cups rolled oats
12 cups oat, alfalfa and or hay chaf
8 cups oat bran
8 cups warm water
8 cups apple sauce
8 ounces molasses

Preheat oven to 325°

Place parchment on baking sheet. In a large bowl, combine all ingredients. Let stand 10 minutes. Add a little whole wheat flour if too sticky. With your hands, form into small patties. Place on baking sheet one inch apart. Bake 35-40 minutes or until light brown and dried out. Cool completely before storing in an airtight container. Makes enough for the whole barn. Dough can be frozen in small packages and baked off as needed.

CHAPATIS & TORTILLAS

2¼ cups flour
 (part whole wheat pastry/white flour
 or all white flour or all whole wheat pastry flour)
2 teaspoons sunflower or other light oil or ghee, *page 57*
pinch of sea salt
1½ cups lukewarm water

Place the flour, salt and oil into the food processor. With the speed on medium, process while slowly adding water. As soon as the dough sticks to itself to form a soft ball, stop adding water. Remove from food processor onto a floured board. Roll in flour and let stand for ten minutes or an hour.

Dust your hands with flour and make 25-30 small balls, about 1½ inches thick. Roll each ball in flour. Using a rolling pin, roll out balls to form 6 inch circles.

To cook chapatis, heat a large skillet or griddle to medium high. Cook each chapati, either dry or with ghee, for about half a minute each side, until it puffs. Serve immediately or keep covered until ready to serve.

Homemade Flour Tortilla Chips

garlic & herb tortillas (or any kind of good quality flour tortillas, or chapatis) cut in strips or wedges
canola oil
salt

In oil about three inches deep, using medium high heat, fry strips until crispy and golden. Drain on paper towel or in a recycled brown paper bag. Salt to taste while still hot.

Buns for Burgers or Hot Dogs

2 tablespoons sugar
2 packets active dry yeast
1/2 cup lukewarm water
2 cups lukewarm milk
2 tablespoons vegetable oil
2 teaspoons salt
6 to 7 ½ cups flour
Egg wash: 1 egg beaten with 1 Tablespoon cold water
sesame, poppy or caraway seeds or coarse salt (optional)

Dough should be quite soft and relaxed to make soft and tender buns. Add only enough flour beyond 6 cups to make the dough knead-able. In a large bowl, dissolve the sugar and yeast in the warm water. Add the milk, oil, and 3 cups of flour to the yeast mixture. Beat vigorously for 2 minutes.

Add the salt and gradually add flour, 1/4 cup at a time, until the dough begins to pull away from the sides of the bowl. Turn the dough out onto a floured board. Knead until dough is smooth and elastic.

Put the dough into an oiled bowl, turning once to coat the entire ball of dough with oil. Cover with a damp towel and let rise until doubled, about one hour.

Turn the dough out onto a lightly floured work surface. Divide into 18 equal pieces.

Shape each piece into a ball. For hamburger buns, flatten the balls into three-inch disks. For hot-dog buns, roll the balls into cylinders, 4½ inches in length. Flatten the cylinders slightly; dough rises more in the center so this will give a gently rounded top versus a high top.

For soft-sided buns, place them on a well-seasoned baking sheet a half an inch apart so they'll grow together when they rise. For crisper buns, place them three inches apart.

Second Rising: Cover with a towel and let rise until almost doubled, about 45 minutes.

Preheat oven to 400°

Just before baking, lightly brush the tops of the buns with the egg wash and sprinkle with seeds, if desired.

Bake for 20 minutes. When the buns are done, remove them from the baking sheet to cool on a wire rack, to prevent the crust from becoming soggy.

Making Ravioli from Scratch

3 cups white flour
1 teaspoon salt
4 eggs
2 Tablespoons olive oil
1 yolk, for egg wash

Combine flour and salt in a bowl. Add eggs 1 at a time and mix into flour. Drizzle in oil and continue to incorporate into the flour until it forms a ball. Sprinkle flour on work surface; knead the dough until smooth and elastic. Wrap the dough in plastic and let it rest for about 30 minutes. Cut the ball of dough in half, cover what you are not using. Dust surface and dough with flour. Form the dough into a rectangle and roll it out thin, thin, thin. The dough should be 1/8 to 1/4 inch thick.

Dust the counter with flour; lay out the long sheet of pasta. Brush the top surface of dough with egg wash. Place 1 tablespoon of cooled filling about 2 inches apart on half the sheet of pasta. Fold the unfilled half over the filling. Using a rolling pin ravioli maker, press the dough together around each bit of filling, or use your fingers to press the dough together. Cut through the pressed dough to make ravioli squares. Make sure the crimped edges are well sealed before cooking so the filling doesn't leak out. If making in advance of serving, dust with cornmeal to prevent sticking.

Cook the ravioli in boiling salted water for 5 to 10 minutes. Ravioli will float to the top when cooked. Gently remove the ravioli from water with slotted spoon. Serve immediately with butter or sauce.

Filling ideas:

4 Tablespoons butter
3 Tablespoons, shallots, finely chopped
1 cup roasted butternut squash puree
salt and pepper
1/4 cup heavy cream
3 Tablespoons grated Parmesan cheese
pinch nutmeg

1 recipe pasta dough,
rolled out into wide ribbons, about ¼ inch thick
12 fresh sage leaves
1 Tablespoon finely chopped fresh parsley leaves

Melt 1 tablespoon of the butter in a heavy bottomed saucepan. Add the shallots and sauté for 1 minute.

Add the squash puree and cook about 2 to 3 minutes. Stir in the cream and cook for 2 minutes. Remove from the heat and stir in 3 tablespoons cheese and nutmeg, to taste. Add herbs. Cool before filling pasta sheets.

Also: finely chopped leftover meats sautéed with onions, etc. or three cheeses (Parmesan, Ricotta & Mozzarella)

Mac & Cheese

2 cups cooked pasta, penne, elbows or bows
1/4 cup butter
1/4 cup unbleached white flour
1/2 teaspoon salt
1/2 teaspoon mustard
1/4 teaspoon pepper
1/4 teaspoon Worcestershire sauce
2 cups milk
2 cups shredded Cheddar cheese

Heat oven to 350°

Melt butter in saucepan over low heat. Stir in flour, salt, mustard, pepper and Worcestershire sauce. Cook over low heat, stirring constantly, until mixture is smooth and bubbly; remove from heat. Stir in milk. Bring to a simmer, stirring constantly. Simmer, stirring, 1 minute; remove from heat.

Stir in cheese. Fold pasta into cheese sauce. Spoon into sprayed or greased baking dish or individual ramekins. Bake uncovered 20 to 25 minutes or until bubbly.

The ultimate comfort food.

More Sweets & Treats

Christmas Plum Pudding

1 cup currants
1 cup golden raisins
1½ cup raisins
1 cup flour
2 cups stale breadcrumbs
1 cup shredded suet
1 cup dark brown sugar
1/4 cup chopped almonds
4 beaten eggs
2 Tablespoon Guinness Ale
juice of 1 lemon
juice of 1 orange
1/2 Tablespoon allspice
1 Tablespoon nutmeg
1/2 cup rum
2 Tablespoons candied fruit peel

Mix all ingredients together in a large bowl and pour into one 7-8 cup English pudding bowl or 2 smaller bowls. Leave at least 1 inch at the top of bowl so that the pudding has room to expand. Cover with two sheets of waxed paper and a layer of aluminum foil. Tie the top tightly around the rim of the basin with string and make a handle so that the pudding can be lifted. Lower the pudding bowl into a large pan of boiling water with a saucer upturned on the bottom. The water should come 3/4 of the way up the sides of the pudding bowl.

Cover and simmer for at least 7 hours. Check that the water does not drop below 3/4 full. Add hot more water if necessary.

Remove the pudding and store in a cool place. To serve, boil pudding for two hours in the same way. Remove the cover and turn the pudding over onto a serving platter. Just before serving, warm a little brandy or rum in a saucepan pour it over the pudding, and light with a match.

Serve with Rum Butter or Hard Sauce.

RUM BUTTER

1 pound brown sugar
1/2 pound butter
1 cup rum
1/4 teaspoon grated nutmeg

Melt butter. Do not let boil. Beat in sugar. Stir in rum, a tablespoon at a time and then the nutmeg. Place mixture into a serving bowl and use when set.

Sealed in an airtight container, Rum Butter will keep for over a month, but DO refrigerate it, as the sugar will recrystallize.

Hard Sauce

1 cup powdered sugar
1/3 cup butter
2 teaspoons rum (or vanilla)

Using the back of a wooden spoon, cream sugar into butter. Add rum (or vanilla). Refrigerate until firm. Serve over hot plum pudding.

Pastry Cream

4 cups whole milk
8 egg yolks
1 cup granulated sugar
10 Tablespoons cornstarch
1/8 teaspoon salt
3 teaspoons pure vanilla extract

In a saucepan, warm the milk over low heat until it steams. While the milk is warming, whisk together the egg yolks, sugar, cornstarch and salt until completely smooth.

Add half of the steamed milk, whisking constantly, to the egg mixture. Add the milk and eggs back into the rest of the hot milk, and heat for 1-2 minutes, stirring constantly, until the custard is very thick. Remove from the heat. Stir in the vanilla extract. Chill before filling pastry. Makes about four cups.

RICE KRISPIES CHOCOLATE BARS

3 Tablespoons butter
1 bag marshmallows
6 cups Rice Krispies
1/2 cup chocolate chips

In large saucepan melt butter over low heat. Add marshmallows and stir until completely melted. Remove from heat.

Add Rice Krispies and chocolate chips. Stir until well coated. Using buttered spatula, press mixture into 13 x 9 inch glass baking dish.

HOLIDAY ORNAMENTS

1 cup salt
2 cups flour
1 cup water
2 Tablespoons vegetable oil
water-based paints

Place dry ingredients in a bowl, add the water and oil, stir until blended. Once the dough holds together, Roll into a ball and kneed it to make a smooth texture.

Place the dough on a cutting-board; roll the dough out a bit thicker than for regular cookies. Cut out the ornaments with cookie cutters or design your own by shaping dough with your fingers.

Don't forget to punch or carve a hole into the top of the ornament for a string to go through to hang the beautiful decoration on your tree! Bake at 200° until hard and dry but not browned - one or two hours.

Cool completely and paint with water-based paints or glue on glitter using white household glue. Thread a string or ribbon through the hole and hang the decoration on the tree.

Ornament ideas: Stars, Hearts, Ducks, Twisted Candy Canes, Trees, Gingerbread Boys & Girls!

Carrot Cake

2 cups flour
1¼ teaspoon baking powder
1 teaspoon baking soda
1 teaspoon cinnamon
1/2 teaspoon salt
2 cups brown sugar
1¼ cup canola oil
4 eggs, beaten
3 cups carrots, grated

Preheat oven to 350°

Sift together dry ingredients. Cream together sugar and canola oil, about two minutes. Slowly add eggs. Blend with dry ingredients. Add grated carrots and blend together. Spray a Bundt pan or baking dish. Pour batter into pan. Bake at 350° for approximately 40 minutes. When cooled, drizzle with a mixture of 2 tablespoons orange juice and about 1/2 cup powdered sugar, or enough to make a thick frosting. This cake is also fabulous with Cream Cheese Frosting or without frosting.

CHOCOLATE / ALMOND OR PEANUT BUTTER BALLS

2 cups peanut or almond butter, smooth or crunchy
1 cup butter, softened
5 cups confectioners' sugar
2 (12-ounce) packages of chocolate chips
(white and/or semisweet)

In a medium-size bowl, combine the nut butter and butter and stir with a wooden spoon, until evenly blended. Add the confectioners' sugar and stir until the mixture has the consistency of dough.

Roll into 1-inch balls and place on a baking sheet lined with parchment. Put the baking sheet in the freezer until the peanut butter balls are solid enough to pick up with a toothpick, about 30 minutes.

Melt the chocolate chips in a microwave or in a double boiler. Insert a toothpick into each peanut butter ball and dip it into the melted chocolate. Set the chocolate-coated balls on a baking sheet lined with waxed paper. Remove the toothpicks.

Immediately place a chocolate or peanut butter chip over each toothpick hole. Cool in the refrigerator until the chocolate has hardened, about 5 minutes.

Makes about 100.

DATE NUGGETS

1 cup date pieces*
1/2 cup almonds or pine nuts
1/2 cup coconut
1/4 cup sunflower seeds
2 teaspoons maple syrup

1/4 cup toasted sesame seeds or coconut or ground nuts, for rolling

Combine the first five ingredients in a food processor and whir until the nuts are crushed and the whole thing forms a kind of sticky dough. Scoop out about 1 teaspoon at a time, forming into balls and roll in toasted sesame seeds. Refrigerate for about an hour.

These keep well in the freezer.

*Or cranberries, or raisins, or any dried fruit

German Chocolate Cake

9inch cake pan with 4 inch sides
Baking Spray

1 4 oz. package Sweet German Chocolate
1/2 cup boiling water
1 cup butter
2 cups sugar
4 egg yolks
1 teaspoon vanilla
2½ cups cake flour
1 teaspoon baking soda
1/2 teaspoon salt
1 cup buttermilk
4 stiffly beaten egg whites

Preheat oven to 350°

Melt chocolate in boiling water. Cream butter and sugar until light. Add egg yolks one at a time, blending well each time. Add vanilla and melted chocolate and mix well.

Sift flour with soda and salt. Add sifted dry ingredients to the chocolate mixture alternately with buttermilk. Don't beat hard – just mix well. Fold in beaten egg whites. Spread batter evenly between three buttered and floured cake pans. Bake at 350° for 35-40 minutes. Cool.

Frosting:

1 cup half and half
1 cup sugar
3 egg yolks
1/4 pound softened butter
1 teaspoon vanilla

Place all ingredients in a saucepan and cook over medium heat for about fifteen minutes, stirring constantly, until thickened.

Add one cup unsweetened shredded coconut and one cup chopped pecans.

Beat with wooden spoon until of spreading consistency.

Spread between layers and on top (not the sides) of cake.

Teas, Drinks & Toddies

Charles Dickens's Very Own Christmas Punch, 1847

In his own words:

"Peel into a very strong common basin (which may be broken, in case of accident, without damage to the owner's peace or pocket) the rinds of three lemons, cut very thin, and with as little as possible of the white coating between the peel and the fruit, attached.

"Add a double-handfull of lump sugar (good measure), a pint of good old rum, and a large wineglass full of brandy—if it not be a large claret-glass, say two. Set this on fire, by filling a warm silver spoon with the spirit, lighting the contents at a wax taper, and pouring them gently in. Let it burn for three or four minutes at least, stirring it from time to time. Then extinguish it by covering the basin with a tray, which will immediately put out the flame. Then squeeze in the juice of the three lemons, and add a quart of boiling water.

"Stir the whole well, cover it up for five minutes, and stir again. At this crisis (having skimmed off the lemon pips with a spoon) you may taste. If not sweet enough, add sugar to your liking, but observe that it will be a little sweeter presently.

"Pour the whole into a jug, tie a leather or coarse cloth over the top, so as to exclude the air completely, and stand it in a hot oven ten minutes, or on a hot stove one quarter of an hour. Keep it until it comes to table in a warm place near the fire, but not too hot. If it be intended to stand three or four hours, take half the lemon-peel out, or it will acquire a bitter taste.

"The same punch allowed to cool by degrees, and then iced, is delicious. It requires less sugar when made for this purpose. If you wish to produce it bright, strain it into bottles through silk. These proportions and directions will, of course, apply to any quantity."

From a letter to an English friend written while Dickens was in Paris. Published in The Dickensian. *London, Chapman and Hall, 1905.*

CHAI SPICES

1/2 teaspoon cardamom
1/4 Tablespoon cinnamon or one stick
1/8 teaspoon black peppercorns
1/4 teaspoon ginger

Grind together. Mix into four quarts water.

Simmer 20 minutes.

Add black tea and milk or coconut milk as desired.

Hot Toddy
A sore throat, cold or flu "calmer"

1 cup boiling water
1/4 cup brandy
1 tablespoon honey
juice of one lemon
cinnamon stick, optional

While boiling the water, place other ingredients in large cup. Pour in hot water. Steep a few minutes. Enjoy while warm. (Ingredients can be doubled and kept warm in a thermos).

A Good Posset

1 cup milk, scalded

Pinch each: cinnamon, cardamom, nutmeg, salt

sugar or honey, optional

Serve in a beautiful cup or mug.

Sprinkle with sweet cocoa powder or cinnamon.

TEAS

Mint (for tummy ache)

Feverfew & Calendula (for headache)

SINUS ANTI-INFLAMMATORY STEAM

Rosemary
Thyme
Eucalyptus
Feverfew
Calendula
Sage
Lavender

Throw a handful of anti-inflammatory herbs into a big pot. Bring to a simmer. The longer it simmers, the more potent the steam. Turn off the heat. Place your nose over the steam and sniff. Slowly. A lot. Breathe in deeply. Breathe out. Breathe in deeply. And so on. No need to place a towel over your head. I find it claustrophobic under there. Repeat steam often throughout the day to help clear sinuses. Herbs can be re-heated several times.

Resources

In Print

The *Honey Baby Darlin'* series - Ginna BB Gordon
  Book One - The Farm
  AmericaStar Books, 2011
  The Gingerbread Farm
  Lucky Valley Press, 2012

Stocking Up - Carol Hupping
Touchstone Books, 1990

The Art of Preserving - Jan Berry and Rodney Weidland
Ten Speed Press, 2003

Save the Males
Reparata Mazzola and Chef Gordon Smith
Save The Males Publishing, 2013

The Letters of Charles Dickens
Pilgrim Edition, Volume Five, 1847-1849, p. 9.

Online:

www.unclejimswormfarm.com

www.growupvertical.com

www.mountainroseherbs.com

www.tomatofest.com

An Epilogue by Ginna: 21st Century Bookbinding

My parents gave me a Little Golden Book called *The Poky Little Puppy* for my third birthday. More Little Golden Books followed, including *Where Is That Poky Little Puppy?*, *Thumbelina*, and *A Television Book of Yoo Hoo*, which had a little dial to turn for pictures of Yoo Hoo, the Elephant, doing various things: showering himself with his trunk-full of water, eating chocolates, petting the dog. The dial is gone now, but not the book.

Elmer and the Dragon, The Velveteen Rabbit and solving *Nancy Drew* mysteries came next. At 9, my older brother, Mark, said, "Go write a book on How to Be Obnoxious in 25 Easy Lessons." I did.

All these books and more are still on my shelves: books about beads, art, ceramics; cookbooks; historical novels and biographies; self-help; spiritual journeys; and geeky things like InDesign manuals; Nolo Press Do-Your-Own-LLC; Do-It-Yourself Plumbing and Upholstery. Dover Books of Design and Clip-Art. Book about books.

I am never without at least one, if not two or three books. My husband David says that when I announce I am "bookless," he gets nervous.

Although I love digital media, I also love the feel of the paper, the inspiration and tease on the cover, beautiful marbled endpapers, sensitively planned photographs, parchment. There will always be books.

During the 70s, I studied everything concerning books and their making: binding; gold tooling; paper making, marbling and decorating; calligraphy. With my Certificate from the Carmel Guild of the Book Arts, I became a bookbinder.

I stepped into my professional cooking years and, during 1995-97, consulted with the Chopra Center for Well Being in La Jolla, and for them wrote my first grown-up book, ***A Simple Celebration, the Nutritional Program for the Chopra Center for Well Being*** (1997, Harmony Books, a Division of Random House).

After an illuminating experience with a prospective publisher, I decided to enter the world of indie-publishing for my next book. I gathered my courage, along with my skills in writing, design and bookbinding, combined them with the talents of my husband and creative partner, David Gordon (design, writing and typography, among myriad others) and created Lucky Valley Press.

To me, the sum of all these things is 21st Century Bookbinding.

And of course, out of that, springs *First You Grow the Pumpkin*, in both print and digital formats.

Measurements & Conversions

Measurement Abbreviations

tsp = teaspoon
Tbsp = tablespoon
fl = fluid
oz = ounce
pkg = package
c = cup
pt = pint
qt = quart

gal = gallon
lb = pound
sm = small
lg = large
ml = milliliter
g = gram
kg = kilogram

Pinches to Spoons

1 pinch = 0.5 gram = less than 1/8 teaspoon
1 dash = 1.18 grams = 3 drops = ¼ teaspoon water
1 milliliter (ml) = 1 cubic centimeter (cc)
1 teaspoon = 4.73 grams = 1/6 ounce of water
1 Tablespoon = 14.18 grams = 3 teaspoons water
4 Tablespoons = 56.70 grams = ¼ cup water
16 Tablespoons = 226.80 gram = 1 cup water

Gallons to Liters

1 gal = 4 qt = 8 pts = 16 cups = 128 fl oz = 3.79 L
½ gal = 2 qt = 4 pts = 8 cups = 64 fl oz = 1.89 L
¼ gal = 1 qt = 2 pts = 4 cups = 32 fl oz = 0.95 L
½ qt = 1 pt = 2 cups = 16 fl oz = 0.47 L
¼ qt = ½ pt = 1 cup = 8 fl oz = 0.24 L

Ounces to Tons

1 ounce = 28.35 grams
16 ounces = 1 pound = 453.60 grams
5 pounds = 2.27 kilograms
25 pounds = 11.34 kilograms
1 ton = 0.91 metric tons
1 metric ton = 1.10 tons

Fluid Ounces to Liters

1 fl oz = 29.63 ml
1 cup = 237.00 ml
1 pint = 474.00 ml
1 quart = 0.95 liter
1 gallon = 3.79 liters

Grams to Pounds

1 gram = 0.04 ounces
1 kilogram = 2.2 pounds
5 kilograms = 11.01 pounds
20 kilograms = 44.03 pounds

Milliliters to Gallons

1 ml = 0.04 fl oz
50 ml = 1.70 fl oz
500 ml = 2.13 cups
1 liter = 1.06 quarts
10 liters = 2.64 gallons

°F–°C Conversions

-10°F = -20°C
0°F = -18°C
32°F = 0°C
68°F = 20°C
90°F = 32°C
212°F = 100°C
300°F = 149°C
350°F = 177°C
400°F = 204°C
450°F = 232°C
500°F = 260°C

-18°C = 0°F
0°C = 32°F
5°C = 41°F
10°C = 50°F
20°C = 68°F
30°C = 86°F
50°C = 122°F
60°C = 140°F
100°C = 212°F
150°C = 302°F
200°C = 482°F

Bar Drink Measurements

1 dash = 6 drops
3 teaspoons = ½ ounce
1 pony = 1 ounce
1 jigger = 1½ ounce
1 large jigger = 2 ounces
1 std. whiskey glass = 2 ounces
1 pint = 16 fluid ounces
1 fifth = 25.6 fluid ounces
1 quart = 32 fluid ounces

Dish Measurements

9x13 inch baking dish = 22x33 cm baking dish
8x8 inch baking dish = 20x20 cm baking dish
9x5 inch loaf pan = 23x12 cm loaf pan = 8 cups = 2 liters
10 inch tart or cake pan = 25 cm tart or cake pan
9 inch cake pan = 22 cm cake pan

Cups to Spoons

1 Tablespoon (Tbsp) = 3 teaspoons (tsp)
1/16 cup (c) = 1 Tbsp
1/8 cup = 2 Tbsp
1/6 cup = 2 Tbsp + 2 tsp
¼ cup = 4 Tbsp
1/3 cup = 5 Tbsp + 1 tsp
3/8 cup = 6 Tbsp
½ cup = 8 Tbsp
2/3 cup = 10 Tbsp + 2 tsp
¾ cup = 12 Tbsp
1 cup = 16 Tbsp
1 cup = 48 Tbsp

Cups to Gallons

1 cup = 8 fluid ounces (fl oz)
2 cups = 1 pint (pt)
2 pints = 1 quart (qt) = 32 fl oz
4 cups = 1 quart
8 cups = 64 fl oz
1 gallon (gal) = 4 quarts = 128 fl oz

Inches to Kilometers

1 inch (in) = 2.54 centimeters
4 inches = 10.16 cm
1 foot = 0.30 meter
5 feet = 1.52 meters
10 feet = 3.05 meters
1 yard = 0.91 meters
1 mile = 1.6 km
50 miles = 80.47 km

Centimeters to Miles

1 cm = 0.39 inches
2.54 cm = 1 inch
5 cm = 1.97 inches
1 meter = 3.28 feet = 1.09 yards
15 meters = 49.21 feet
1 km = 0.62 mile
1500 meters = 4921.25 feet
50 km = 31.07 mi

Lucky Valley Press
Carmel, California
WWW.LUCKYVALLEYPRESS.COM

Body Text: Optima
Headers: Copperplate

www.ingramcontent.com/pod-product-compliance
Lightning Source LLC
Chambersburg PA
CBHW050553300426
44112CB00013B/1899